How To Win Your Audience With Bombproof Humor

To: Win Pendleton
My mentor and friend
for many years

To: Heather
My daughter who makes me laugh
and brings me so much joy

Karl E. Righter, DTM

copyright 2010

Contents

Preface   5

The Messenger & the Mentor   8

1. Humor in Communication   12

   The importance of humor in communication
   Myths about humor
   15 ways humor helps the speaker
   The saving grace

2. What's so Funny?   18

   The joke
   The difference between wit & humor
   Perspective
   25 types of humor
   How to tell a funny story
   Make it fit
   Let them laugh
   Make a difference
   Stage time

3. Laugh at Yourself...Others Are!   33

   What's your problem?
   Winning your audience with self-effacing humor
   Find your signature story
   Savers
   Don't be predictable

4. The Theory of Bombproof Humor   40

The difference is in the expectations
The theory of bombproof humor
The challenge of humor

5. The Element of Surprise   42

Don't announce your humor
The testimonial letter
The quick strike
Keep them in suspense

6. Tell a Story, Make a Point   46

Get personal
Stay on point
Great expectations
Turning point
The payoff of originality

7. Make it Believable   52

Faking sincerity
Illustrative examples
Longer stories
Reruns
Make it believable

8. Practice Makes Perfect   58

9. Win Them Over Early   61

Event promotion
Opening strategies
Use your imagination

10. Leave Them Laughing — 72

The best way to end your speech
Examples of humorous closers

11. Avoiding the Pratfalls of Speaking — 77

Types of humor to avoid
Turn disaster into laughter
Lackluster applause
Dealing with hecklers
Losing your place
Disclaimers
But what if you bomb?
The bottom line

12. Where's the Humor? — 85

Be a student
Choose your environment
Finding humor
Writing original humor
Become a student
Stage time

13. Special Occasions — 95

Master of ceremonies
The celebrity roast
The contest speech
Giving a toast
Giving a eulogy
Speaking to young audiences
Religious groups
Other special events

About the Author — *114*

Preface

"Humor in public speaking is like the salt, spices, and herbs in cooking. The proper seasoning can change a tasteless dish into a gourmet's delight. Humor can turn a dull speech into a resounding success."

- Winston K. Pendleton
Speaker, author, humorist

Humor is one of the most powerful skills you can employ as a public speaker, presenter, or meeting chairperson to regale your audience with wit and leave them laughing.

Humor breaks down communication barriers, warms up your audience, holds their attention, uplifts their spirits, and makes your message more memorable. Humorous stories or illustrations can also reinforce important points and make your audience more receptive to your ideas.

Unfortunately, humor is one of the most challenging speaking skills to master. Poorly delivered, it can detract from your presentation. Used inappropriately, it can make you look like a clown. The difficulty of delivering humor smoothly and professionally, coupled with the fear of "bombing," keeps many speakers and presenters from incorporating this powerful tool in their presentations.

The Purpose of This Book

This book is not intended to turn you into a stand-up comedian. Instead, it is an indispensible guide to learning how to find, create, and deliver humor effectively within the context of a prepared presentation.

In this book, based on my humor workshop, *How To Win Your Audience With Bombproof Humor*, you will learn fifteen ways humor can improve your presentations or speeches, 25 types of humor and when to use them, five key rules for using *bombproof humor*, excellent sources for finding humorous material, proven methods of personalizing stock humor and making it sound genuine and believable, humor for special occasions, and much more!

Comedian Jerry Seinfeld once noted the irony that the fear of public speaking ranks ahead of the fear of death on most lists. He remarked, "If that statistic is true, then at a funeral, the guy giving the eulogy would probably rather be in the casket!"

My belief is that the fear of "bombing" when attempting humor is as terrifying for many as is the fear of public speaking, or even flying! Presumably for those timid souls, the ultimate terror then would be to have to fly somewhere to give a humorous speech.

Bill Gove, past president of the National Speakers Association, was once asked if you have to be funny to be a professional speaker. He replied, "Only if you want to get paid." Humorist Darren LaCroix adds, "Funny equals more money!"

Of course, we may not all want to get paid as speakers, but we all want to get results. Accordingly, everyone can benefit from an ability to use humor effectively. The good news: you don't have to be naturally funny or have a sharp wit to be an entertaining speaker, presenter, or meeting chairperson. The key is understanding how humor works, and being prepared.

Who Said it First?

It has been said that there is no original humor...that all gags are rewrites or embellishments of older gags. This book contains many quotes and references, and I have valiantly attempted to give credit when possible. This is a challenge, because over the last 30 years of writing, studying humor, and speaking professionally, I have heard many of the same jokes or quotes attributed to a number of different speakers or authors.

Many of the books I have referenced for humor in the past don't even bother to credit anyone for the laugh line as it has been used by so many different people! So, who said it first? We can never be sure. Accordingly, when I attribute a quote to a specific source in this book, that may simply mean that he or she was the person I happened to hear it or read it from at that time and can find no other definitive original author.

Let's Get Started

So get ready to embark on a journey of self-discovery and personal growth. What? You're not sure you can learn to become an entertaining speaker? Don't be intimidated. This book will help you step-by-step. And don't give up. My first attempt at a humorous speech generated one laugh, and the master of ceremonies got that one introducing me!

The Messenger and the Mentor
Acknowledgements

"I have seen what a laugh can do. It can transform almost unbearable tears into something bearable, even hopeful."

- Bob Hope

There wasn't a lot of laughter in my home when I was growing up. With a strict military father and an absentee mother working two jobs, I was emotionally stunted as a child. My only friend in high school was a popular student named Melvin Riley, star of the high school track team, president of his Junior Achievement company, and a self-professed heart throb to the ladies. He was a charmer so extroverted that I was rendered irrelevant in social settings when we were together.

Fortunately for me, a reprieve from my isolation came during my senior year in high school. Introverted and so insecure that I probably couldn't have led a Sunday school class in silent prayer, I was persuaded by Melvin to join his Junior Achievement company. It was scary at first, but our group was friendly and supportive, and that experience offered a much needed emotional stretch for me.

Since our Junior Achievement company was in the running for several year-end awards, including *company of the year* and *president of the year*, I attended the organization's annual awards banquet during the month prior to my graduation. In a room packed with 1,500 students, friends, and family members at the Statler Hilton Hotel in downtown Dallas, our company garnered the top award, as did our president, Melvin. But that wasn't the highlight of the evening for me.

The Messenger

The master of ceremonies at that affair was Pierce Allman, a well-known local celebrity who later became the radio voice of the SMU Football Mustangs. For over an hour-and-a-half that evening, Pierce Allman had the audience in the palm of his hand, entertaining us with his infectious wit and uproarious humor. He poked fun at himself, our organization, and other popular personalities in the room. The mood was exhilarating! For a child who had so little to laugh about, I was absolutely spellbound. Even today, decades later, I still vividly remember how for one brief moment the sadness and loneliness of my childhood were wiped away by waves of laughter.

In every life there is a messenger who awakens us and helps us discover the music within...our own unique gift or talent. Pierce Allman had the right remedy that evening for what was ailing me, and that remedy was laughter. At some level, I must have realized that if I could someday make people laugh and also inspire them, then perhaps I could put light in people's faces as Pierce Allman had done that special evening. And thus began a subconscious calling to become an ambassador of good will and someday make a difference in people's lives through the power of the spoken word...and laughter.

The Mentor

Once I had a sense of purpose, I became the proverbial student ready for the teacher to appear. It didn't take long after graduating from college to find one.

I joined a Toastmasters club in Orlando, Florida, shortly after being stationed there as a green second lieutenant in the Air Force. It wasn't my idea to join a speaking club. Because I was the new Base Information Officer and would be required to represent the Air Force and speak at community events, my commanding officer ordered me to join Toastmasters and learn how to communicate more effectively.

Just as I had experienced years earlier in Dallas, I subsequently heard at a Toastmasters conference a charismatic keynote speaker, Winston K. Pendleton, renowned author, humorist, and radio personality, who entertained us for over an hour with his funny stories and humor. Once again, I was transfixed and inspired by a speaker who made me laugh. I knew immediately that I had found the mentor who could help me become an entertaining professional speaker. Best of all, he lived locally and was a frequent contributor and friend to Toastmasters.

In 1978, I took a chance and asked him to coach me as I prepared for Toastmaster's Annual Humorous Speech Contest. I couldn't believe it when he said "Yes!" Winston Pendleton, one of the most popular after-dinner speakers in America, was going to take the time to tutor me on the basic rules for successful storytelling and how to capture and keep an audience's attention with humor.

That year I made it all the way to division level in the Humorous Speech Contest. The next year, I advanced to district. Finally, in 1980, after years of personal study, workshops, mentoring, continued involvement in Toastmasters, listening to countless cassette programs, and Win Pendleton's invaluable guidance, I won Toastmasters International's highest level of the Annual Humorous Speech Contest at a regional conference in Jeckyl Island, Georgia.

My dream of becoming an entertaining professional speaker was officially launched with that victory. After that, I became more in demand as a keynote speaker and trainer, and I was frequently asked to present humor workshops at district, regional, and international Toastmasters conventions.

These workshops were billed *How To Win Your Audience With Bombproof Humor,* and they were based upon proven humor techniques that I learned from Win Pendleton and expanded upon through research and study. I collaborated with Win in the early years of presenting this workshop and was honored to have him as a guest contributor on many occasions.

Standing on the Shoulders of Giants

Isaac Newton once said of his successful discoveries, "If I have seen a little further it is by standing on the shoulders of giants."

Winston K. Pendleton was a giant in the rarified stratosphere of entertaining keynote speakers and gifted published authors. It was a privilege and an honor to learn from him and to call him a wonderful friend for many years until his passing. I have dedicated this book to Win and have included many references to his ideas throughout. The cover art for this book is a tribute to Win, who graciously gave me permission to use it in my workshop materials over the years and on the cover of the book I promised him I would write someday.

Pierce Allman was the messenger who awakened in me the idea that I could someday become an entertaining speaker. But it was Win Pendleton who was the mentor who showed me the way.

(1)
Humor in Communication

"A smile is the shortest distance between two people."
- *Victor Borge*
Comedian

Humor has been called the universal language. A laugh in any culture is exactly that...a laugh, a signal that one is enjoying the moment. Reader's Digest says, "Laughter is the best medicine - the perfect prescription for what ails us."

Unfortunately, we don't laugh nearly enough. Studies show that the average four-year-old laughs over 400 times a day, while the average adult laughs only about twelve times a day - even less if they have a four-year-old!

We've become too stressed and sensitive. I was teasing my administrative assistant recently about her filing skills and her ability to lose massive amounts of information in a single day. She replied, "Don't knock it! These little defects kept me from getting a better boss!"

Yes, America needs to laugh more, and as speakers or presenters, we can provide an essential service if we can inform, uplift, *and* entertain our audiences!

The Importance of Humor in Communication

What are the marks of an effective speaker, one who is in demand and gets invited back to an organization time after time? According to John Kinde, author of *Humor Power Tips*, "He or she first connects with their audience by being in the moment, not in their speech! They converse in a conversational style with their words, and their eyes."

The bottom line is, great speakers do more than make a speech...they make a difference by bringing a message that people need to hear, in an effective style that commands the audience's attention. The good speakers always find out in advance of their presentations what are the frustrations of the group to whom they will be speaking. By doing this homework, they are able to make a connection by speaking to those frustrations and putting them in perspective.

These are all fundamentals of good communication, but the really effective speaker adds the additional dimension of humor to make his or her message memorable. The importance of humor in communication becomes clearly evident during the course of a typical Toastmasters meeting or speech contest. For example, if you have two speakers of equal talent, both well prepared, informative, articulate, and succinctly organized, the speaker that usually wins the trophy is the one that adds effective humor and entertains the audience.

Myths About Humor

It is important to dispel a few myths about humorous speaking. The first myth is that one has to be naturally funny to be an entertaining speaker. That is not true. I was not born with a great sense of humor. As I mentioned in the previous chapter, I have had to work hard and receive coaching to develop the skills and techniques necessary for recognizing and using effective humor. More important than a great sense of humor in speaking is informed preparation and practice.

The second myth about humorous speaking is that you have to be able to remember jokes. While this ability may be valuable when called upon for impromptu remarks or during typical social interaction, this gift is not a requirement for the prepared speaker who uses humor to enhance his or her message. Again, preparation and rehearsal trump an ability to remember jokes.

Finally, there is the myth that you have to be a stand-up comedian to be a humorous speaker. As you will learn, *bombproof humor* depends upon the element of surprise. Stand-up comedians are expected to get laughs, but no such pressure or expectations exist for the inspirational keynote speaker who has a message that can be enhanced with humor.

15 Ways Humor Helps the Speaker

Win Pendleton said, "Humor is the single most powerful card in the hand of a public speaker - it can make the difference between a winning speech and a lost evening. Humor can win many a trick for you if you take the time to learn how to play it properly."

Here are 15 ways in which humor helps a speech, from the moment you are introduced until the time you step down from the dais:

The Opening

The most crucial part of any speech is the first minute immediately following your introduction. Here are several ways humor helps you start off strong:

1) Attract Attention - There are often distractions that you will have to overcome in the opening of your presentation. People may be engaged in conversation or moving their chairs around to get more comfortable. At a luncheon or dinner event, people may still be finishing their meal, or you may even be introduced while some of the servers are still clearing the tables. In such situations, nothing will grab the attention of your audience as effectively as a well-crafted opening humorous story. The resulting wave of laughter will momentarily overshadow any distractions and rivet attention on you.

2) Create Expectancy - After an opening laugh, your audience is now eagerly anticipating that they will be entertained, and they will be anxiously awaiting your next humorous story. Create a humorous title for your presentation, such as I did with my keynote address, *Laugh at Yourself, Others Are*, and add humor to the written introduction that you prepare for the program chairperson, and the anticipation of a memorable talk will build even before you get to the lectern!

3) Break Down Barriers - There is often a pre-existing communication barrier between speaker and audience which opening humor can quickly dismantle. Self-directed humor goes even further by taking the audience off the defensive and showing them that you don't take yourself too seriously!

4) Build Rapport - When you and your audience are both having fun, there is a natural bonding that occurs during a pleasant shared experience. Building rapport boosts your chances of success and insures that your message will be seriously considered.

5) Relax Your Audience - Once you have created a roomful of friends, you have accomplished the additional goal of helping the audience to relax. Laughter eases tensions and makes your audience more receptive to your ideas.

6) Relax Yourself - Nothing is more encouraging for a speaker than to hear an audience roar with laughter. Warming up your audience with humor and building immediate rapport is a tremendous confidence-builder that also relaxes you and makes you more effective.

The Body

Once you feel that you and your audience are warmed up and enjoying the experience, there are several other ways in which humor can help you throughout the body of your speech:

7) Dramatize a Key Point - A humorous analogy, story, or illustration can help clarify a key point and make the premise more vivid and memorable. Humor provides a second opportunity to make the same point in a different way, thus increasing understanding.

8) Hold or Regain Attention - Periodic humor in a presentation maintains the air of expectancy that you established in the opening and keeps the audience focused upon you and your message. If some listeners have drifted away into their own thoughts or have been distracted by a neighbor's comment, the laughter of others will usually bring them right back. They will not want to miss your next funny story.

9) Keep Audience Alert - Like the blind javelin thrower at the Olympics, laughter keeps the audience alert! It increases heart rate and boosts alertness, making your audience less likely to become lethargic and inattentive. As Win Pendleton liked to say, "When members of your audience are on the edges of their seats, in anticipation of being entertained, they are much less likely to fall asleep in that position."

10) Help Audience Follow You - Humor helps break the listener's preoccupation with your previous point or their own tangential thoughts and serves as an excellent transitional tool that helps your audience follow you from one topic to the next.

11) Uplift Spirits - Dr. Ralph Smedley, the founder of Toastmasters International, said, "We learn in moments of pleasure." Psychologists believe it is virtually impossible to laugh and feel depressed at the same time, so uplifted spirits lead to better learning environments. After the laughter is when many "Ah Ha!" moments occur.

12) Make Tedious Material More Enjoyable - Humor adds spice to long presentations or extended technical information. Noted motivational speaker Zig Ziglar used humor approximately every seven minutes during his three-hour seminars to make his presentations more entertaining and memorable.

The Conclusion

Many speakers find it difficult to wrap up their speeches in a compelling manner. Here again, humor can play several important roles in helping you bring your presentation to a perfect conclusion:

13) Prepare Your Audience for Your Conclusion - The correct funny story can signal that you are now approaching for a landing. Humor helps prepare your audience to receive your important summary or call to action.

14) End Speech on an Upbeat Note - When your call-to-action incorporates humor, the impact of your closing message is intensified. The audience thus leaves in a positive frame of mind and will be more inclined to endorse your point of view. There is no sweeter sound to a speaker's ears than the sound of applause *and* laughter as he or she departs the lectern!

15) Ongoing Goodwill - The entertaining speaker will be the one that is remembered, and recommended! As previously emphasized, a great speaker does more than make a speech...a great speaker makes a difference! And humor can make a great speech even better!

The Saving Grace

There is one other way in which humor can come to the aid of a speaker. It can mask imperfection!

Perhaps your message didn't resonate with your audience the way you had hoped for reasons beyond your control. For example, maybe the preceding program has run long and you have been asked to shorten your speech on the fly. This can rob you of continuity or force you to leave out important information. Or perhaps there was a failure of the microphone, unusual distractions, or you weren't at your best. In these situations, humor can be your saving grace by allowing you to still create a favorable experience for the audience and get you and the program chairperson off the hook.

Speech Trainer Patricia Fripp talks about this concept in her classes. She suggests that a rapport with the audience covers flaws. When giving a talk, whether you're getting laughs or motivating the audience, don't worry about being perfect. It's nice to be prepared, but perfection is not a requirement. In fact, an occasional stumble makes you a real person. Audiences identify with and like someone who is real. And when people like you, it's easier to be funny.

Good communication is essential to understanding. A sense of humor makes good communication even better.

(2)
What's so Funny?

"Humor is tragedy separated by space and time."
- Charlie Jarvis
Speaker & humorist

How many times have you said, "Someday, we'll look back at this and laugh." Hopefully not right after you've just attempted a humorous speech. The point is, a sense of humor helps us put things into perspective. Ann Landers said, "A sense of humor can help you overlook the unattractive, tolerate the unpleasant, cope with the unexpected, and smile through the day." We can help our audiences see their life's challenges in a different light if we can first lighten their mood through humor. To do that, we need to understand how humor works. So let's begin with a few definitions:

The Joke

According to Webster's Dictionary, "A joke is a brief narrative story with a humorous, climactic twist." As an analogy, when telling a joke, you are leading your audience in a certain direction, like a train going down the tracks... and then you cause a train wreck! The art of humor is knowing when and where to have the wreck!

For example, consider the quip about the businesswoman who examines her lottery ticket one morning at work and discovers she has all six numbers! She realizes this ticket is worth a fortune. Her first instinct is to call her husband who is home watching TV. "Honey, I'm looking at a winning lottery ticket that's worth a fortune! Pack your bags for a trip!" "Great! Where to?," he replies. "I don't care! I just want you out of the house by the time I get home!"

Humorist Darren LaCroix, the Toastmasters 2001 World Champion of Public Speaking, says comedy is connecting two things that the audience does not see. The lottery ticket story works because you have led the audience down a path that suggests the husband and wife will take a vacation together to celebrate their good fortune. The punch line, or train wreck, is the disclosure that only the deadbeat husband will be going away.

If a joke bombs, it may be because the audience doesn't have the right frame of reference. For any number of reasons...poor joke set-up, wrong theme for this audience, etc., the direction of the train is not apparent to the audience. You can't derail a train that's not going anywhere.

The Difference Between Wit and Humor

As humorist Charlie Jarvis once explained, "Wit *punctures,* humor *pictures!"* What did he mean? Wit is intellectually upbeat language that surprises and delights us. It is short, snappy comedy, a one-liner, a pun, or joke. Wit is the unexpected, quick, and humorous combining of contrasting ideas or expressions.

While wit *punctures* with its sharp focus, humor, on the other hand, *pictures!* Humor is an entertaining story (not necessarily a joke). It can be an unpleasant situation told in a playful way. It can even be a joke that has been rewritten and developed into a major presentation point. In essence, humor paints vivid pictures.

Perspective

Darren LaCroix said, "Humor is in the eye of the beholder." It's true. What may seem funny to one person may not register at all with another. People with a sense of humor see things differently.

For example, comedian Demetri Martin once noted that one person may view swimming as a sport, while another person may believe you only do it to not die! The comedian noted, "Perhaps the only way to know which is which is by what the person is wearing at the time. Pants? Uh Oh! Swimming suit? That's better!" It's a matter of perspective.

The challenge for speakers is to try to use field-tested humor that clicks with a high percentage of people, and to use *bombproof humor* techniques that will be explained later in this book. Remember, a person doesn't have to laugh out loud to be enjoying themselves! Smiles are always welcome.

Another consideration is the size of an audience. A small turn-out of 10 - 15 people is a tough audience for any humorous speaker. Sure-fire humor that consistently works for you in larger venues may fall flat in a small room where individual members of the audience may feel self-conscious about laughing out loud. Again, the use *bombproof humor* techniques will avoid any perception of bombing and the resulting embarrassment.

25 Types of Humor

Humor is not a one-dimensional technique. There are a wide variety of styles and types which should be understood in order to use the right strategy at the right opportunity. Here are 25 of the most frequently used types:

1) One-Liner - This is the most common form of humor...short and peppy. Example: "I don't jog because it makes my beer foam up." Humor doesn't get more succinct than that! A word of caution...too many one-liners and you cross the line from speaker to comedian, undermining the gravity of your message.

On the other hand, if not overused in your presentations, and if they are relevant to your message, one-liners can catch your audience by surprise and generate some unexpected laughter. Sometimes they can be rewritten and expanded into longer stories that fit many of the following styles.

2) Rule of Three - Basic speech training teaches the rule of three for building understanding. This theory suggests that important points should be made more than once, ideally in three different ways, to enable the listener to internalize the information.

The rule of three in humor works a little differently and is an effective humor style. Essentially you have a three-part story: the first two parts of the humorous story set the tone and direction, like the train going down the track, and the third part, the punch line (or train wreck), throws a curve and provides the element of surprise. Example: "My new neighborhood has everything a single person could want...nearby parks, a jogging trail, and a liquor store on the corner." The third item in the list is always in sharp contrast to the set-up items, but it is consistent with the theme of the story.

3) Exaggeration/Understatement - This technique takes a normal issue or topic to an extreme point of view, or dramatically minimizes it. Example of exaggeration: "He's been married so often, he now qualifies for group alimony." Example of understatement: "In honor of David Smith's service this year as president of our association, the Board of Directors, by a vote of five to four, has chosen to honor him with the following award..."

4) Humor by the Numbers - Statistics can be misleading, as evidenced by the sad case of the hunter who drowned crossing a stream that *averaged* only three feet deep! Numbers can also be boring, or lacking in clarity. Humor by the numbers can transform boring statistics into something more informative, or at least more entertaining by providing some levity and a frame of reference. Example: "These are tough times for the airline industry. Last year Delta lost $100 million, and that was just luggage!" That line is also an example of exaggeration, and when you can combine two or more humor styles into one quip, it adds to the impact. Another example of making statistics fun: "A recent study shows that every eight seconds, some woman, somewhere in the world, is giving birth to another baby. Personally, I think we should find that woman and stop her."

Numbers themselves can be humorous. "Zillionaire" is a funny term for a rich person. "Zilch" or "goose egg" are funnier than saying "none."

5) Satire - Satire is often used in business and politics to make fun of important people or institutions that may need a reality check. The well-known expression, *the pen is mightier than the sword,* speaks to the power of this form of humor to create political unrest. Jay Leno often uses satire in his nightly monologues. An example of Leno's wit: "The Department of Homeland Security is getting tough on immigration. They just announced that they deported 280,000 illegal aliens last year, and they have threatened to deport them again this year!"

6) Housekeeping - This type of comedy is used in the opening minutes of a presentation to warm up the audience and establish common ground. The humor typically references the hotel or venue, the food or service, the meeting arrangements, local news that is relevant to the event, your written introduction, or the event itself. As master of ceremonies, Johnny Carson once opened his Academy Awards remarks with, "Welcome to the Academy Awards…20 minutes of wit and scintillating entertainment, spread over the next four hours!" Another example: "When I asked the program chairperson how big a room I'd be working tonight, he said, 'It sleeps 500.'"

7) Reverse - With this style of humor, the speaker establishes a clear direction and expectation with the joke's set-up, convincing the audience that they already know the outcome of the story. He or she then creates the exact opposite conclusion. In other words, the reverse is a classic train wreck in which the train actually stops and backs up, crashing into the train behind it!

Example: "A positive identification was made in a police line-up today that wrapped up a case. When one of the five suspects saw the female victim being escorted in, he yelled, 'That's her!'" Another example: "An air quality alert was issued today in the city of Chernobyl, Russia. Apparently the wind from Newark was blowing their way!" In each of these illustrations, the outcome of the story is the exact opposite of what you expected.

2005 Toastmasters World Champion Lance Miller had a great reverse in his winning speech as he described his first date: "There we were, parked on Lovers Lane, and I was monopolizing the conversation talking about me. It was me, me, me…my, my, my…finally, I got tired of talking about me. I said, 'Enough about me. I want to hear from you. What do you think about me?'"

8) Parody - This type of humor alters just enough of a popular song, quotation, person, event, or idea that the target is still readily identifiable, and yet much funnier in its revised form. Examples: *Time wounds all heels, Where there's a will, there's a relative, The early worm gets picked off by the bird,* and, for the singing impaired: *The Star Mangled Banner.*

9) Pun - A pun is a play on words, sometimes on different meanings of the same word, or on similar senses or sounds of different words. Puns are often referred to as both the lowest form of comedy and as intellectual humor. They frequently elicit groans from the audience. There are two reasons: first, puns suggest that the speaker is trying to be clever; and second, a pun generally comes so quickly that the audience doesn't have time to grasp its humor. Still, a really clever pun can be funny. Example: *Does the name Pavlov ring a bell?* Or, *If you don't pay your exorcist, you get repossessed.*

10) Self-Directed Humor - Self-deprecating humor takes your audience off the defensive and let's them know you don't take yourself too seriously. There is a whole new world of opportunities for humor when you can laugh at yourself. An example of self-directed humor: "My personal trainer told me to wear loose-fitting clothes to workouts. I told him that if I had loose-fitting clothing, I wouldn't need to work out!" Another example from comedian Jim Gaffigan: "I come from a very big family...nine parents." We'll explore in detail the power of self-deprecating humor in the next chapter, *Laugh at Yourself, Others Are.*

11) Double Meanings - As humorist John Kinde points out, "Many words have double meanings, so that word play often hinges on taking figurative expressions literally." Kinde offers an example: "When Abraham Lincoln was accused by his political opponents of being two-faced, he aroused chuckles (and good will) among electors by replying that, if he did indeed have another face, he would surely wear it!" One of my personal favorite plays on words is: "The short fortune teller who escaped from prison was reported to be a *small medium at large.*"

12) Combinations - A humorous effect can be achieved by combining two disparate ideas, especially when one of them is a common expression. Example: "Most long-winded speakers can be stopped...when push comes to shove." Another example: "It was love at first sight...but then I took another look." During an introduction that I once received at a celebrity roast, the roastmaster said, "Two cities claim the birthplace of our honoree: Palm Beach, and Buffalo. Palm Beach claims he was born in Buffalo, and Buffalo claims he was born in Palm Beach." Combining the illogical premise that one person could have two birthplaces makes this gag work well.

13) Call-Backs - This technique builds upon a funny premise by referring back to it later in your speech, sometimes often, but especially in your conclusion. In a contest speech entitled *The Music Within,* I opened with a funny story about my first exposure to "hillbilly" music. Then, in the conclusion, I tied back to that story with another, more complimentary reference to country music that illustrated my continuing enlightenment in the area of music appreciation. John Kinde calls this process "bookending." The bookends (humorous stories or references) are similar, that is, they match.

Note that a call-back doesn't have to link with a funny story or joke. You can plant seeds during your presentation and refer back to them later, often for comic effect. For example, in the opening of Ed Tate's 2000 World Championship speech, *It Was Just One of Those Days*, he describes waiting in line at the airport to rebook a flight that he was going to miss because of a delay caused by the airline's new baggage policy. While waiting, he is mentally rehearsing his strongly worded complaint that he will voice to the unfortunate airline representative. However, the person ahead of him beats him to the punch with an almost identically worded complaint, thus stealing his thunder. This represents a call back to the previous set-up and is ironically funny even though the "seed" was not.

A call-back can also capitalize on a funny remark by a previous speaker on the program, even from the day before, because it taps into the audience's common frame of reference. Such humor shows that you are spontaneous and in the moment. This application of the call-back is explored in more detail later under *Observational Humor.*

14) The Topper - A first cousin of the call-back, the topper is a strategy where one joke sets up another of the same theme, providing an opportunity for an even better follow-up laugh. Essentially you build on the momentum of the first laugh and take advantage of the elevated mood of the audience. The second, or even the third topper, also creates the impression that you are quick on your feet, as though you just thought of those additional quips.

In the music speech referenced previously, I used this technique to talk about the challenges of playing the piano professionally: "One night, an older gentleman came up to the piano, put $5 in my tip jar, and said, 'Would you play Moon River?' I replied, 'Sir, you're not going to believe this, but that's the song I just got through playing!' He said, 'Oh, thank you,' and took back his $5!'"

In this example, the first joke was the disclosure that I butchered Moon River so thoroughly that the gentleman who requested it didn't even recognize it. That always gets a laugh. The topper was the ad-on line, or insult to injury, that he took back his $5 tip!

Of course, a topper may not be planned. It could actually be a spur-of-the-moment afterthought, making it even more fun for you as well as the audience.

15) Sarcasm - According to Wikipedia, sarcasm is a sharp, bitter, or cutting expression or remark; a pointed jibe or taunt. It is not a good idea to use this form of humor until you have established a bond or connection with the audience as it may be considered offensive. For example, after a joke bombs, saying, "If these jokes are going over your head, you may want to stand!," will probably not be well received.

A softer version of sarcasm can involve irony, such as saying to a lazy worker, "Don't work too hard!" As Wikipedia points out, the use of irony introduces an element of humor which may make the criticism seem more polite and less aggressive.

16) Malapropisms - According to Webster's dictionary, a malapropism is a humorous misuse or distortion of a word or phrase. An example would be former Yankees manager Casey Stengel's classic line, "If people don't want to come to the ball park, nobody can stop them."

Another form of malapropism is the use of a word sounding somewhat like the one intended but ludicrously wrong in the context, such as substituting "ovulation" for "ovation," or "psychotic" for "psychic." Sometimes a malapropism is obviously unintentional, making it even funnier.

Changing a single letter in a word can provide a hilariously new version as these following malapropisms illustrate: *Intaxication: The euphoria at getting a tax refund, which lasts until you realize that it was your money to start with; Sarchasm: The gulf between the author of sarcastic wit and the person who doesn't get it:* and, *Reintarnation: Coming back to life as a hillbilly.*

One of my favorite examples of a malapropism involved a friend of mine who sent a greeting card from Hawaii to his wife in Orlando while he was away at a convention. It was the typical card from Hawaii with the palm trees and the hula dancer on the front. Inside he wrote a brief message but inadvertently left the letter "e" off the word "here." As a result, after opening the card with the hula dancer on the front, the wife read his message: "Wish you were *her.*" They laughed about that right up until the divorce.

17) Observational Humor - As a speaker or master of ceremonies, you have ample opportunities to add spontaneous humor to the program by observing the things that are going on around you, and looking at them from a humorous perspective.

In Chapter Nine, *Avoiding the Pratfalls of Speaking*, you will learn strategies for turning chaos into comedy, from issues like dishes crashing to the floor, flopping or squealing microphones, hecklers, botched introductions, to cell phones going off, etc.

Other applications of observational humor include adding humorous perspective to previous comments that preceded your part of the program. For example, a previous speaker may have used the quote, "You can lead a horse to water, but you can't make him drink." Later, you might refer back to that quote and add a postscript, "but you can put salt in his oats and make him thirsty!" This is also an example of a call-back as previously discussed.

One of my best ad libs ever using observational humor occurred at a district Toastmasters conference in Boca Raton, Florida, while I was serving as the MC. This was back in the days when the Saturday night closing banquet typically ran very long due to lengthy speeches, a plethora of awards to everyone but the food servers, and even more announcements than awards. As the hour approached 11:00 pm with no end in sight, I paused and said, "Fellow Toastmasters, you will note on the front of your programs that the date of this event is October 25, and if we hurry, we can still make it!" This observation resonated with the weary audience and the laughter turned into applause, a sign that I had not only said something funny, but that I had also secured universal agreement of my point.

18) Acronyms - You can use acronyms as a form of humor during a presentation. An acronym is an abbreviation that is formed using the initial letters or components of a phrase or name, i.e., IRS (Internal Revenue Service), CIA (Central Intelligence Agency), etc. There are many acronyms that are unique to your particular audience, and they offer an excellent opportunity to make a connection with them early.

The humor strategy is to change one or more of the words that the acronym represents into a funnier version. For example, ETA is an acronym for "Expected Time of Arrival," but for many punctually challenged individuals, it could represent "Expected Tardiness Allowance." Similarly, the acronym CEO (Chief Executive Officer) might become "Clueless Executive Officer" during a celebrity roast.

19) Oxymorons - When a statement or phrase is perceived as incongruous, it is also likely to be experienced as humorous. Examples of oxymorons (contradictory expressions) include: *jumbo shrimp, plastic silverware, freezer burn, non-dairy creamer, first runner-up, rolling stop, airline food, etc.*

20) Ludicrous Perception - This type of humor is based on absurdity, such as exaggerated physical mannerisms, unusual apparel, slapstick comedy, clownlike behavior, etc. In other words, the humor is more visual than verbal.

For a classic example of this humor type, refer to Darren LaCroix's opening in his World Championship speech, described on page 70, in the chapter *Win Them Over Early*.

21) Props - A prop is any object held, used, or pointed to by a speaker or presenter for use in expanding the impact of a story, point, or theme. It can also be a hat or article of clothing, a stick-on tattoo, a clown nose, etc. Whereas words can quickly become boring, a unique prop is hard to ignore. On page 43 of Chapter Five, *The Element of Surprise,* I describe a funny testimonial letter that I use as a prop to make a point early in my keynote speech, *Laugh at Yourself, Others Are.*

Another prop I use to humorous effect in that same speech is a hand-written sign I purportedly find in the restroom prior to the program. I hold the sign up, mention that some wise guy had taped it to the hot air dryer in the men's room, and then I read it as follows: "For a preview of Karl Righter's speech, press button."

You can also enlist members of the audience in advance or during your presentation to use as human props. This can include arranging for someone to hand you a bogus announcement which you then read aloud, or, planting funny questions with audience members to ask during question-and-answer sessions. It is recommended to keep props hidden until you are ready to employ them.

22) Quotations - A funny quotation is essentially *bombproof humor* as you are quoting someone else's observation to reinforce a point in your presentation. There are myriad sources of quotations in books and on the Internet. Always identify the source when possible.

23) Insults - This type of humor is best used during a celebrity roast and is described in detail in the chapter *Special Occasions.* It is rarely appropriate in any other type of serious presentation.

24) Anachronisms - According to Wikipedia, an anachronism is an error in chronology, especially a chronological misplacing of persons, events, objects, or customs in regard to each other. An example would be Christopher Columbus using a GPS device to find America.

25) Definitions - This is a fun type of humor in which you can make up your own definitions of terms for comedic effect. Robert Frost was responsible for this example: *Jury - twelve persons chosen to decide who has the better lawyer.* Here's another good example: *Flabbergasted - being appalled by discovering how much weight one has gained.*

How to Tell a Funny Story

Now that you understand different humor styles, have you ever wondered why one speaker can entertain an audience with a funny story, and another person, telling the same story, will bomb? The answer is usually in the delivery.

A classic analogy of this premise is the story about a gentlemen's cigar club. These men had been socializing for so many years that they knew everyone's favorite jokes by heart. Eventually, they numbered the jokes to save time. For example, one gentleman would say "#43!" and the group would laugh uproariously. A new gentleman was added to the group, and he quickly picked up on the efficiency of numbering his jokes. One night, he belted out his favorite, "#22!" No one laughed. Then he shouted "#16!" Again, no response. Later that evening he asked one of the seasoned members why his jokes didn't generate any laughter. The older gentleman replied, "Some people can tell a joke, some can't!"

Regardless of the storytelling technique, if an audience responds with laughter, you can be certain that four basic humor principles have been followed (which will be explored in more detail in the later chapters on delivering *bombproof humor*): First, you must preserve the element of surprise. Second, your story must seem believable. Third, it must be delivered correctly according to the guidelines of humor style outlined previously. Fourth, you must learn your story so well that you will be able to tell it without ever making a mistake or forgetting the punch line.

Consider the humorous story about the church elder who was always complaining to the minister about what was wrong with the church. One day he confronted the minister and said, "Why don't we have a plaque in our foyer like the Baptist Church across the street, honoring those members of our congregation who have died in the service?" The minister replied, "Which service, the 9:30, or the 11:00?"

This story meets the first three criteria of a successful joke: 1) the punchline is well concealed, 2) the story is believable, and 3) the comedy style (self-directed humor at the expense of the minister) is well executed. The fourth criteria, how well the story is delivered, is the deciding factor.

Learn the strategy of delivering *bombproof humor* outlined in the following chapters, and you can take your success to an even higher level. Being able to tell a funny story is not a gift. It is a technique that can be learned and perfected.

We will go into more detail on how to tell a funny story in subsequent chapters.

Make it Fit

Win Pendleton wrote: "When you are looking for a story to fit your speech, you should always consider what people laugh at, and what they don't laugh at. Be sensitive to their frustrations and do not trivialize them through comedy."

"On the other hand," Win said, "people do laugh at individuals who get into predicaments or embarrassing situations due to their own stupidity, gullibility, conceit, or overeagerness. Comedian Jack Benny was a marvelous storyteller. When you laughed at him, you were laughing at the always-trying-to-be-clever person who usually loses out."

As suggested earlier, when looking for a funny story, the best person to play the role of the embarrassed dunce is you. Be sure that you think it is funny and that the humor can be easily appreciated.

The good news: humor is ageless. As long as a story fits smoothly into your speech, the age of the joke is unimportant. Many speakers today are getting belly laughs with stories that were told by Abraham Lincoln, Winston Churchill, Will Rogers, and other historic personalities. And you can be sure that those celebrities didn't think up all of their own stories either.

A good rule to follow when delivering a funny story is to build upon your premise and make every sentence point directly to the eventual punch line. Make everything you say in the build-up relevant to the point of the story. When you write and rework your stories, be sure they complement your personality. Craft them with the magic element of surprise. And keep them short and to-the-point.

Let Them Laugh

One of the biggest surprises to the aspiring humorist is his or her first big belly laugh after a joke. It catches them by surprise, and they often end up stepping on their laughs. Even experienced speakers step on their laughs. What does that mean? It means the speaker did not allow the laughter to die down before continuing their speech. When you resume speaking while the audience is still laughing, you are subconsciously telling them, "Stop laughing...I have something more important to say!" Well, there's nothing more important than allowing your audience to enjoy themselves.

Make a Difference

The rules of effective humor are very similar to the rules of good communication. First, you need to have a dialogue with the audience, not a monologue. The more interactive and engaging you can be, the more of a connection you will forge. Using rhetorical questions, favoring the word "you" more than "I" or "me," and speaking directly to individuals while seeming to include everyone, are great rules of effective communication.

Most of all, you must always quickly answer the question every member of an audience has at the beginning of your speech..."What's in this for me?" Tell them early, promise them a payoff, then deliver, and you will make a difference! And remember, your presentation is not about you or how funny you are - it is about what others take away from your message.

Stage Time

I will occasionally hear after a speech how fortunate I was to have been born with a sense of humor. In reality, I was not funny until after years of studying humor and being coached by others. When you see an entertaining speaker, you are seeing the end result, not the long process needed to get there! This book is designed to dramatically shorten that process.

Another way I learned was by speaking as often as possible. World Champion speaker Darren LaCroix's mantra for becoming a better speaker is "Stage time, stage time, stage time…grabbing every opportunity to speak and learn." During his learning process, Darren would drive an hour-and-a-half each way every night for a mere five minutes of stage time at a comedy club in Portland, Maine. His friends told him he was stupid. Years later, because of this dedicated process, Darren became a World Champion and highly paid keynote speaker. Then his friends told him how lucky he was. Apparently, he noted, "You can go from stupid to lucky if you work hard enough! So if your friends call you stupid, you're probably on the right track!"

The same premise applies to delivering humor effectively. You will only become more adept by not shying away from humor. Don't be afraid to fail. Relegate stage fright back to the era when people were afraid to travel by Wells Fargo!

(3)
Laugh at Yourself...Others Are

"God blessed America with a marvelous sense of humor, but we like to laugh at the other guy."
- Will Rogers

It's true! Other people's gaffes crack us up! But when *we* do something embarrassing, it's not so funny. But it could be even funnier, for ourselves, and others, if we could learn to lighten up! To be able to do so is a sign of self-confidence and enlightenment.

In our personal lives, self-deprecating humor can diffuse tense, interpersonal situations that could easily escalate into heated discussions or arguments. For example, I was watching a football game one afternoon when my wife came into the living room and said in a confrontational voice, "It's obvious you love football more than me!" I smiled and replied, "Yes, but I love you more than basketball!" This spontaneous act of accountability and humility on my part caught her off guard and caused her to chuckle. The effect of not being argumentative and defensive turned a potential fight into a shared laugh.

Most of us don't take criticism very well. It makes us defensive, or we reciprocate in kind. We don't like to be put down. However, Eleanor Roosevelt pointed out, "No one can make you feel inferior without your consent." So, a better approach to criticism or a put-down is to see the humor in the situation. Woody Allen was once criticized for the modest box office returns of his movies. He replied, "If my films don't show a profit, I know I'm doing something right."

There are really only two good responses to criticism: either learn from the criticism and thank the person for the feedback, or, if it is unwarranted, laugh it off. Psychologist Dr. Wayne Dyer used to bristle when he would receive a letter criticizing one of his books. What was he supposed to do with the negative input...recall all of his books and fix them? Instead, he decided to respond with humor. He drafted a form letter that said: "I am sitting in the smallest room of my house, with your letter of criticism before me. Soon, it will be behind me." You may have to think about that one for a moment!

Similarly, in response to a critical letter, humorist Charlie Jarvis had his own canned response: "Dear sir: I thought you should know that some moron has stolen some of your stationery and is using it to send out idiotic correspondence."

What's Your Problem?

Do people often tease you about a certain physical or personality characteristic? Do you get upset when this happens? Why not join the fun and start kidding yourself! Identify the things that people tease or insult you about, and then use them to your advantage. When you do, it takes all the wind out of your tormentor's sails. What pleasure will they have by continuing to make fun of you if you're having more fun with it than they are?

Humorous Speaker Jeannie Robertson is sometimes characterized in her promotional materials in this manner: "Barefooted, and with her hair 'mashed' down, she is six-feet-two, the tallest Miss America contestant ever from the state of North Carolina." Obviously she was teased unmercifully over the years about her height. Finally, she decided to see the humor in her situation and laugh at herself. She tells the story of sitting next to a gentleman on a commercial airline flight. Upon getting out of her seat to deplane at her destination, the man blurted out loudly enough for all to hear, "Wow! You're tall!" She replied, "Gosh, I wasn't when I got on the plane. Must be those peanuts!"

We worry too much about what others think of us. Wayne Dyer puts our preoccupation with this into blunt perspective with his philosophy: "You would stop worrying about what others think of you if you only realized how seldom they do!" My personal philosophy, and the title of this chapter, is *laugh at yourself, others are!*

Winning Your Audience With Self-Effacing Humor

For a speaker or trainer, self-deprecating humor is the highest form of levity because it disarms your audience and shows them that you have a healthy sense of humor! Best of all, you'll never run out of material when you are able to kid yourself. It's the safest form of humor you can use. And feeling safe with humor is comforting.

It has been said that every joke has a victim or target. The problem is that if you choose an inappropriate target, you could offend someone, perhaps a lot of people. Note that politically incorrect humor can be rewritten and told upon yourself, making it non-confrontational to the audience. Uncomfortable situations can also be diffused in this way. For example, instead of attacking your audience for a lackluster round of applause, you could say, "Thank you for that heart-warming round of indifference - apparently you've heard me speak before!" Ask yourself if a particular joke you are considering could be taken personally by an individual, group, organization, or demographic profile. If so, switch targets! Rewrite the story using self-deprecating humor and paint the bulls-eye on *your* back.

Kidding yourself is particularly effective in the opening of your presentation as it immediately signals that this is going to be fun, especially fun at your expense! For example, in a past speech about mental health, *Are You Normal?*, I opened with the following self-deprecating story:

> *Have you ever visited a mental health institution? I have! During a time when I was gathering information for this speech, I visited a mental asylum and asked the director how is it determined whether a patient should be institutionalized. "Well," said the director, "we fill a bathtub, then we offer a teaspoon, a teacup, and a bucket to the prospective patient and ask him or her to empty the bathtub." "Oh, I understand." I replied. "A normal person would use the bucket because it's bigger than the spoon or the teacup." "No," said the director, "a normal person would pull the plug. Do you want a bed near the window?"*

Professional speaker Patsy Dooley is a large woman who uses that reality to her advantage. For example, sometimes when she takes the stage and has to speak from behind a microphone on a pole, she may open with, "Can you see me behind this thing?"

Ronald Reagan, as president, was a master of self-deprecating humor. At one particular press conference, he revealed that he was now wearing a hearing aid. One reporter asked, "What kind is it?" President Reagan looked at his watch and replied, "10:35."

Darren LaCroix, early in his winning World Championship speech, *Ouch*, won over his audience of 2,000 by poking fun at his entrepreneurial ineptness when he stated, "After four years of business school, I went for the American dream...I bought a Subway® sandwich shop. I don't want to brag, but, in six short months, I took a $60,000 debt, and I doubled that debt! That's right, I turned Subway® sandwich shop into a non-profit organization." In this example, Darren combined self-deprecating humor (doubling his debt) with a topper (non-profit organization). As previously noted, when you can combine two humor styles into one story, the humor effect can be magnified.

Find Your Signature Story

Humorist John Kinde points out that professional speakers who are in demand are often known for their "signature stories." These are original, entertaining personal experiences that offer a moral or lesson learned. Kinde says, "In a great story, the message is built around drama, challenges or obstacles, relationships, or strong characters." I have also found that these stories are great opportunities for incorporating self-deprecating humor.

Signature stories need to be about significant events in your life, personal, or professional. When speaking, I have several from which I can choose, depending upon the message and the audience. One theme, which I alluded to in the previous chapter, centers around the challenges I faced as a musician. Another involves the pressures of starting my own business years ago, an advertising agency. Following is an example of one of my best signature stories, a story about role models, from a contest speech entitled *The Sins of the Father*:

Many years ago, I was listening to Harry Chapin's hit song "The Cat's in the Cradle," and the words gripped me like no other song had ever done before. As many of you may recall, that song is about a father and his son...and in many ways, it is about every father and his son... because throughout the song, the son keeps promising his dad..."I'm gonna be like you, Dad, you know, I'm gonna be like you!"

Isn't that an awesome responsibility for parents...to know that their children are going to try to emulate them...good or bad! Personally, I wanted to be like my dad. He seemed strong and invincible. I never saw him afraid. I never saw him cry. Unfortunately, I never saw him much at all.

Because of his emotional detachment, I was so starved for attention that I would intentionally get into trouble just to have some interaction with him. One night I was up in my bedroom and I called down to my dad to bring me a glass of water. He yelled back to go to sleep. Again I called down for water and his tone became more agitated: "Go to sleep, son, or I'm going to come up there and whip you!" Suddenly, a light went on in my head, and I yelled: "Dad, when you come up to whip me, could you bring me a glass of water?"

He never did come up that night, but once again I said to myself, "I'm gonna be like him some day!" Years later, as I listened to the words of that song again, it finally dawned on me...I had turned out just like him. To paraphrase the song, "I too had a child who wanted to play...but I had planes to catch and bills to pay!"

And when I was home, I was just as emotionally distant as my father had been. I could usually be found watching an endless line-up of sporting events on television. My wife once joked that if she ever left me, I probably wouldn't even realize it unless they ran a story about it on ESPN!

One day, my daughter, Heather, came running up to me while I was watching yet another football game and excitedly said: "Daddy! Daddy!

Mommy said she wants to be cremated!" Without even glancing away from the TV I replied, "Tell her I'm busy right now...it will have to wait!"

This is an emotional story for me, and it is even more poignant in the context of the rest of the speech. Note that this particular story has several humorous, self-effacing lines that break the tension of the dramatic material and make the topic more memorable and entertaining.

Find your own signature story, one that is uniquely yours and which distinguishes you from other speakers. It may take a lot of soul-searching to find the perfect story that characterizes you, but the rewards will be worth the effort. And don't be shy about poking fun at yourself in your story.

Savers

In the chapter *Avoiding the Pratfalls of Speaking*, I share some humorous recoveries you can use when things go wrong. These snappy comebacks are referred to by some speakers as *savers*, and they work best when they poke fun at yourself. Here are a few funny savers I have used when I have had a problem with Power Point:

I'm sure this fiasco will be on You Tube before I even get home tonight!

Is there anyone in the audience who would like to finish this presentation? I'm supposed to be at Happy Hour right now.

These slides must belong to the next speaker. I don't recognize them!

Savers are an acknowledgement that you are human, and your audience will appreciate your willingness to take ownership of your situations. Savers are valuable opportunities to laugh at yourself.

Don't Be Predictable

I have often said, "It is a lot easier to get a new audience than a new joke." The reality is that we have our favorite funny stories, and because they have been well received in the past, we continue to use them. However, they become less humorous to audiences that have heard them before.

It is a good idea to keep scripts of the speeches you have given to particular groups, so that if you are invited back in the future, you will be prepared to deliver new material. For some speakers, that is a challenge, but if you are a fan of self-deprecating humor, you should have no problem finding new laughs.

(4)
The Theory of Bombproof Humor

"What would you do if you knew you could not fail?"
- Robert H. Schuller
Pastor & Inspirational Speaker

The fear of bombing when attempting humor keeps many good speakers from becoming great speakers. I have known brilliant corporate trainers who have valuable information and experiences to share with their clients, but they are excruciatingly tedious in their delivery. They manage to keep busy because what they know is in such demand, but their potential to become nationally acclaimed speakers is limited because of their unwillingness to risk using humor in their presentations. One trainer whom I tried for years to encourage to incorporate humor in his workshops finally quit the profession because of lukewarm reviews.

When I talk about the concept of *bombproof humor*, I get skeptical looks and resistance. The naysayers always remind me that highly paid comedians like Jay Leno, David Letterman, and others bomb almost every night during their monologues. So what are the odds, they ask, that we lesser mortals can deliver surefire humor? The answer is simple.

The Difference is in the Expectations

There is a big difference in expectations between the comedian who is delivering stand-up comedy and the motivational speaker who uses humor selectively and effectively to enhance his or her message. The pressure is on the comedian to consistently deliver one zinger after another, and when a gag falls short, it is glaringly obvious. The motivational speaker, on the other hand, is not expected to deliver a steady stream of belly laughs. In other words, with the comedian, the focus is humor. With the motivational speaker, the focus is the message, hopefully enhanced with humor. This is why the entertaining speaker is in demand.

So how does one reconcile the fear of bombing with the need to be entertaining? The solution is the use of *bombproof humor*. What exactly is that?

The Theory of Bombproof Humor

Bombproof humor is a speech organization strategy in which key speech or presentation points are so skillfully reinforced with funny stories that the humor supports the premises of the points regardless of whether it gets any laughs or not.

Speaker and trainer Andy Dooley implores his speech workshop students to "Tell a story, make a point...tell a story, make a point!" When a humorous story also makes a point, it stands on its own and has merit independent of its humorous perception. The premise of *bombproof humor* is simple: *If your audience doesn't know you are telling a joke, how can it bomb?*

As you will learn in subsequent chapters, when you connect with your audience and let them know you care about them, then it's OK if your humor doesn't always get laughs, because that's not the point. Making a point is the point!

The Challenge of Humor

The challenge of being entertaining is to camouflage your humor, although some of you have been doing too good a job of that. Accordingly, the next nine chapters are devoted to helping you incorporate the proven strategy of winning your audience with *bombproof humor.*

Robert Schuller asks, "What would you do if you knew you could not fail?" Hopefully you would try to become a more entertaining speaker!

(5)
The Element of Surprise

"A story to me means a plot where there is some surprise. Because that is how life is - full of surprises."

- Isaac Bashevis Singer
Nobel Prize-Winning Author

Do you remember going to the circus as a child and laughing at the antics of the clowns? If you had the good fortune, as I did, to be seated in the first couple of rows next to center ring, you may remember one shtick where a clown runs toward the audience with a bucket of water and heaves it into the shocked, screaming crowd. I certainly screamed! Then my screams turned into laughs when I realized, as those around me did, that there was no water in the bucket...just confetti!

Now imagine if the ringmaster had prepared us for this ploy with the announcement, "All right, you folks over there in the cheap seats, get ready! Bozo is going to run toward you and pretend to throw water on you, but don't worry, it's just confetti." Obviously the element of surprise is ruined, and the payoff is rendered moot. But you do get to keep the confetti!

Don't Announce Your Humor

The same deflated result can happen to you as a speaker when you announce that you are about to tell a funny story. Remember, the power of humor is in the element of surprise, the train wreck, and when you warn the audience that you're about to tell a joke, part of the surprise has already been let out of the bag. They know the train is supposed to come off the tracks before you even get it rolling. So it better be a good train wreck!

How often have you said during a speech or presentation, "That reminds me of a funny story!" Or, "On the way to the meeting tonight, a funny thing happened!"

Win Pendleton taught me: "A funny story should be an integral part of your speech and not a separate item that seems to be tacked onto it. When it is time to deliver the story, tell it without any preliminary hemming and hawing. Move into it smoothly, with no giveaway signals. Do it just the way a star quarterback makes a sneak hand-off. His action is so slick that it appears effortless. His aim is to hand off that ball so skillfully that his movement is unnoticeable. Just let him fumble the ball a bit and he's in trouble. The same is true with storytelling. Sometimes it takes only one fumble to cost you the game."

In fact, six things can happen when you announce humor, and five of them are not good: 1) you lose the element of surprise, 2) you have focused the audience's attention on the joke instead of your talk, 3) instead of letting them decide for themselves, you have challenged the audience by telling them that this is going to be a funny story, 4) you have increased the pressure on yourself to deliver because of the heightened expectations, and 5) you have set yourself up to bomb!

There's that dreaded word "bomb" again! Recall from the previous chapter that the premise of *bombproof humor* is that if the audience doesn't know you are trying to tell a joke, how can it bomb? So why warn them!

Of course, this rule is not absolute. Announcing humor doesn't mean you won't get any laughs. Remember we said six things can happen when you announce that you are about to tell a joke, and five of them are not good. The sixth outcome is that your audience may still laugh, but when they knows it's coming, your joke is no longer bombproof. It's also just a joke and not serious content.

The Testimonial Letter

In the opening of my *bombproof humor* workshop, I talk about the challenge of learning to think funny and seeing the humor in various situations. I note that the fear of using humor and bombing holds many speakers back. Then I offer the attendees hope by suggesting that my *bombproof humor* system eliminates bombing, and thus it eliminates the *fear* of bombing! I then pose a rhetorical question, "Does this system actually work? Allow me to share a testimonial letter from a recent attendee of my workshop..." I then remove the letter from my coat pocket and read it aloud:

> *Karl, all my life I've been the butt of everyone else's jokes, but I've never been funny myself. I think I inherited a deficient humor gene from my father. In fact, my friends laughed at me when I told them I was going to take your humor workshop, but I took it anyway, and they're not laughing now!*

Note how I moved seamlessly from my point (that *bombproof humor* works) into reading a seemingly plausible testimonial letter that contained a surprise twist, or play on words. The element of surprise is preserved. By the way, I get a great add-on laugh, or "topper" when I end the letter with, "...and they're not laughing now. Signed, _____?_____ (name of well-known personality within that group who is not considered funny)."

The Quick Strike

Sometimes you can hit the audience so quickly with a laugh that they don't see it coming at all. For example, in my contest speech *The Music Within*, I open with, "Do you remember a time when you first stumbled upon a country music station and heard some guy with a twangy voice and a fiddle singing, *How can I miss you if you won't go away?*" Wham! An immediate payoff that the audience wasn't expecting. I didn't announce it, and I barely even set up the punch line, but it got my speech off to a fast start. The quick strike works just as well as when you more deliberately affect a smooth transition from a point to a funny story.

In his 2001 world championship winning speech, *Ouch*, Darren LaCroix weaved humor effortlessly into his message of always getting up when you fall down. Here is an excerpt:

> *I was listening to a tape of Brian Tracy, a great speaker. He asked the question, "What would you dare to dream if you knew you wouldn't fail?" I struggled for an answer...then...BING! It hit me! I would be a comedian! But you have to understand my background...I wasn't*

funny, I wasn't a class clown. In fact, the first time my brother ever laughed at me was when I told him I was going to be a comedian...ouch!

Note that there was no tip-off that the funny line about Darren's brother was coming. He just said it, and it got a huge laugh. Remember, the power of humor is in the element of surprise, the train wreck. Announcing in advance where and when the train is coming off the track steals your thunder.

Keep Them in Suspense

Humor is challenging enough without tipping off your audience that you are about to attempt it. Why not surprise them and expertly weave it into your message!

You can certainly break this rule and still get a laugh. Just realize that when you do, your humor is no longer bombproof!

(6)
Tell a Story, Make a Point

"I use the rule of three to make important points. If one of those repetitions is a humorous story, I have added a powerful dimension to my speech."

- Bob Richards
Olympic Champion & Speaker

The second rule of *bombproof humor* is: *use a funny story that reinforces a key point*. This is an extension of the first rule, *don't announce humor*, as it preserves the element of surprise and appears to be a logical continuation of your speech.

Repetition is a proven learning strategy. Important points should be made several times, in different ways, to nail down the lesson. A humorous analogy can add an additional dimension to your message by providing entertaining support for your premise. When your audience is laughing and enjoying themselves, they are more alert and receptive to your ideas. As speaker Mary Hirsch once said, "Humor is a rubber sword - it allows you to make a point without drawing blood."

Best of all, when humor makes a point, it stands on its own merits...it adds value to your speech whether it gets a laugh or not. Any laughter that results is a bonus and not the point of the story. By definition, it is bombproof because the audience doesn't know you are trying to be funny. You are simply telling a story and making a point.

For example, assume that you are trying to make the point that we sometimes get so wrapped up in our own affairs that we forget about other people, even those closest to us. To reinforce this point, you might consider the story about the man who showed up at a sold-out football game and gently placed a woman's coat and an extra ticket on the seat next to him. The spectator behind him asked, "Are you saving that seat for someone?" The man said, "No, it would have been for my wife, but she's passed on." "Oh, I'm so sorry to hear that," the spectator said. Then he added, "Gosh, why didn't you give that extra ticket to a friend?" The man turned around with a surprised look on his face and said, "All my friends are at the funeral."

The point which this funny story reinforced is that we all sometimes forget about the people who are important to us. This guy just did it bigger, and that makes it funny while making a point. We will explain how to make that and other similar stories bombproof in the next chapter.

Get Personal

Personal stories are a powerful way to make a point come to life. Remember that people came to hear you share your experiences, not to hear you relate several jokes you found on the Internet. As John Kinde reminds us, "People love stories. Throughout time, stories have been a powerful tool to communicate points and make them memorable. We care more about a person when we know his or her story. We want to identify with them. We want to like them." And as we learned in a previous chapter, self-deprecating humor endears us to our audiences and helps us make that personal connection.

Can you make fun of your defects? Can you share the embarrassing moments of your life and make people laugh uproariously? If you can do that while reinforcing a key point of your speech, you will have made an indelible impression and improved understanding. Because of the captivating power of personal stories, the points you make will have more impact and will be remembered long after you are finished.

Sometimes an attendee at one of my workshops will say, "I don't have any humorous personal stories. Nothing funny happens to me!" Actually, that's probably not true. There is humor all around us. What she really meant to say is, "Nothing *seems* funny to me!" And that just indicates that this person hasn't learned to look at life situations from a different viewpoint. She hasn't yet developed her humor perspective. But with study and coaching, she can! Anyone who applies themself can learn to think funny.

Speaker Herb True once attributed humorist Charlie Jarvis' sense of humor to a great recall of stories from his past. "That's true," Charlie replied, "but my stories work because there are experiences in *your* past that they tap into." In other words, the personal stories of others help us relate to our own frames of reference. We say to ourselves, "I can relate to that!"

The challenge with this approach is getting past the reluctance to open yourself up to laughter at your expense. Inspirational humorist Andy Dooley was taken advantage of years ago in New York City's Times Square when he got drawn into a game of Three-Card Monte, a classic short con game in which the victim, or mark, is tricked into betting a sum of money on the assumption that he can spot the money card among three face-down playing cards. Andy lost all his cash that fateful day and was too embarrassed to talk about it for 15 years! After joining Toastmasters and learning the power of self-deprecating humor and story-telling, he incorporated that emotionally humiliating experience into a hilarious seven-minute contest speech that enabled him to win the Toastmasters Annual District Humorous Speech Contest only two years after joining the organization!

Remember, humor is tragedy separated by space and time, painful things told playfully. Don't wait 15 years to finally see the humor in a painful situation. A sense of humor is life's tension-release mechanism, and it will win your audience.

Stay on Point

While a humorous story or analogy can reinforce a key point and aid retention, irrelevant humor can detract from your message and call attention to the fact that you are trying to be funny.

For example, let's say you make a statement in your speech that the economic situation has negatively affected just about everybody, and you then attempt to reinforce that point with, "The economy's so bad, Snow White had to lay off six of her seven dwarfs."

Since Snow White is a mythical character, this choice of story has two disadvantages when attempting *bombproof humor:* 1) you have lost the element of surprise because the audience knows the minute you mention Snow White that this is a joke, and, 2) since it is an obvious joke, it doesn't add the gravity you want when you have just made a serious point. You may get a laugh with this joke, but when your audience realizes it's not a serious point, not only have you failed to add substance to your previous point, but your joke is no longer bombproof either. You have increased the pressure on yourself to deliver because of the revelation that you are trying to be funny.

A better follow-up to "The economy's so bad..." would be something along the lines of, "...I got passed over for a promotion, and I own the company!"

Great Expectations

Here is a brief example of how a personal story can reinforce a key point in a speech, and entertain the audience with *bombproof humor* at the same time. This excerpt is from a contest speech entitled *Great Expectations*, in which I shared personal stories of how important role models are in our lives, and how my father's great expectations for me put added pressure on me as a young boy:

I was in awe of my father. He seemed larger than life to me! Literally larger than life - he was 6'4, and as a little boy, I had to run to keep up with his long, purposeful strides. He played football at Syracuse University. He was a war hero, a college professor, and ultimately, a senior engineer on the space program that sent men to the moon! Oh, did I mention, he also played Moses in the school play!

Not surprisingly, because of his achievements, he had great expectations for me, just as your fathers probably had for you! So there we were one day, father and son, having a chat about my future. I remember him speaking to me in his stern, military tone: "Son, you're starting high school Monday, and it's time to get serious about your life, especially if you're going to be an engineer like your dad!"

Well, I didn't want to be an engineer! I struggled with this pressure, and not wanting to confront my father, I quivered in silence for what seemed like an eternity. Finally, I said, "Dad, I don't want to be an engineer. I don't have the personality!" He replied, "I know, son, you're a natural!"

This personal story unfolded in two parts. First, I established why I held my father in such high regard by citing his numerous accomplishments. I then reinforced that image with the humorous observation, "Oh, did I mention, he also played Moses in the school play!" In the second part of the story, I described how I felt pressure to follow in my father's enormous footsteps and become an engineer. Then I used humor to illustrate my realization that resistance was futile: "Dad, I don't want to be an engineer. I don't have the personality!" He said, "I know, son, you're a natural!"

Note how much the preceding story supported my premise that role models and expectations can exert tremendous influence in our lives as children. Without the stories, I would merely be offering lofty platitudes with little emotional impact, personal investment, or entertainment value. The payoff of such a hollow effort would only come when I eventually uttered the hopeful phrase, "In conclusion..."

Turning Point

Here is a another example of how a poignant and entertaining personal story can reinforce a key point in a speech. This excerpt is from a another contest speech of mine entitled *Turning Point*, in which I shared the story of my younger brother, Pete, who after only a year in the profession of selling life insurance, reached a critical juncture in his career, a turning point that came to him like a thunderbolt:

> *Philosopher Yogi Berra once said, "When you get to a fork in the road, take it!" But which one? In the career of every professional, there comes a turning point, a fork in the road, where we either learn a fundamental truth about why we are in the profession we chose, or, we take a less enlightened path and lead what Henry David Thoreau referred to as "Lives of quiet desperation."*
>
> *A number of years ago, my brother, Pete, came by my house one afternoon and excitedly announced to me: "Karl, I'm a salesman!" I said, "What do you mean? You've been selling life insurance for almost a year!" He said, "Yes, but I haven't been a salesman! I've been an*

order-taker! You and I both know that the only people I've sold insurance to are the immediate family, and I couldn't even sell you, my own brother!" I said, "Don't take that personally! You know my philosophy about life insurance. I don't own any, because when I die, I want it to be a real tragedy!"

Pete laughed, but added, "Regardless, I haven't been a salesman, I've been a solicitor! But I'm a salesman now!" I said, "Tell me what happened!"

What followed then was Pete's powerful story of how he realized on a sales call to a high school buddy and his wife and baby that he was *selling* to people, when he should have been *serving* them. The lead-in above, containing a funny quote from Yogi Berra and another humorous line about life insurance, reinforced the point that my brother was at a crossroads in his professional career while setting up his career-changing revelation that followed.

The Payoff of Originality

Another important benefit of sharing the above stories with my audiences: those stories were not jokes. Therefore, this was original humor, assuring me great peace of mind that there was little chance that the audience would have heard them before.

Conversely, if you are one of several speakers at a conference and you are relying on jokes instead of stories, you really have to listen to all of the other speakers to be sure they don't use one of your gags.

Tell a story. Make a point. Tell a story. Make a point. Tell a story. Make a point. Not only do personal stories bring clarity and authenticity to your message, they serve as catalysts for *bombproof humor,* making your message even more memorable.

(7)
Make it Believable

"The secret of success is sincerity. Once you can fake that you've got it made."

- Jean Giraudoux
French Dramatist

Obviously Jean Giraudoux said that with tongue in cheek, but there is a lot of relevance to that premise when using *bombproof humor*. In the previous chapter, we discussed the importance of incorporating original, personal stories to reinforce key points of your speech or presentation. When you do, you will seem fresh and authentic, and there will be little chance your audience will think that they have heard the story before or that you are using canned humor.

Sometimes, however, you don't have the right personal story to make a point and get a laugh. What to do then? You could turn to a joke book that has humor organized by categories and find the punch line you need, but then you run the risk of tipping your hand that you are trying to be funny by using generic comedy.

The challenge then is to make canned humor appear believable! This third rule is an extension of the first two rules, *don't announce humor,* and *use humor that reinforces a key point*, as it preserves the element of surprise and appears to be a logical continuation of your speech. Conversely, launching into an obvious gag like the Snow White joke, or, "There were two camels that went skydiving," is as obvious a contradiction to *bombproof humor* strategy as is announcing that you are going to tell a joke.

Tailoring humor to flow smoothly with your material positions it as a logical extension of your speech. Sure, you can still get a laugh with the camel joke, but why compromise an otherwise professional presentation with slapstick comedy. Realize that when you do, the humor is no longer bombproof.

Faking Sincerity

It has been said that great speeches are not written, they are rewritten, many times, each version an improvement over the previous iteration. The same premise applies to making canned humor sound believable...it has to be rewritten, tried out on an audience, and possibly rewritten again!

That's because most stock humor found in joke books or other sources is so formulaic and predictable that it would stand out in a speech and call attention to itself, thus ruining the surprise factor that is so important to *bombproof humor*. Context is critical.

Real personal experiences are always preferred, but if you must add stock humor, select a joke that reinforces the point you are trying to make. Then use the following four-step formula to personalize the joke and seamlessly adapt it to the logical flow of your speech so that it adds value rather than serving as a distraction:

1) Set the Scene - Rewrite the joke and make it believable by giving the characters and locations in the story actual names, and setting the situation during some definitive period of time. Use exact numbers rather than approximate figures to enhance believability. Consider putting yourself in the story, or someone you know. Establish the situation as though it really happened.

2) Build the Story - Use vivid word pictures to bring the story to life in graphic detail. Act the part, using as many communication techniques as appropriate, such as gestures, vocal variety, props (remember my testimonial letter?), audience involvement, etc. Become the story yourself. Appeal to the audience's senses of sight, sound, taste, touch, smell, etc.

3) Emphasize the Punch Line - Resist the tendency to rush the punch line. Timing and dramatic impact are essential. In the first two steps, you have successfully set up a believable situation and moved the audience in a certain direction. Now, the punch line should provide a humorous, climactic twist, so be sure to pause for dramatic effect, and clearly state the punch line. The punch line should be at the very end of the joke so you don't step on your laughs...and be sure to allow the laughter to run its course before resuming your talk.

4) Practice, Practice, Practice - The effectiveness of *bombproof humor* is dependent upon its smooth execution and the polished delivery of the punch line. Timing is everything in humor. Rehearse your story so you don't need to read it. Make it sound conversational. Practice these four steps, incorporating some stock humor from a joke book.

Illustrative Examples

Using this four-step formula, any joke can be modified to seem original. Here is a typical joke about marriage from a joke book:

Stock Joke - *The secret of a happy marriage is not trying to run your spouse's life...or your own!*

Clearly this is a weak gag, with a predictable punch line. It needs to be rewritten, expanded, and personalized to have a better chance of adding value, and, as a bonus, a laugh. Consider this adaptation of the one-liner above, which I used several times when I was married to point out that a happy marriage is no fluke:

Personalized - *My wife Carol and I were pretty excited and feeling like real pros recently when we made it to our fifth anniversary, until we realized that her parents were about to celebrate 40 years together! This past weekend, when we were at their home for dinner, I decided to ask my father-in-law, "What's the secret of a long and happy marriage?" He pulled his glasses down, looked me squarely in the eyes, and said with sincerity, "It's simple, son! I don't try to run Maggie's life...and I don't try to run my life either!"*

Here's another example where I took a stock joke and rewrote it for a speech on the travails of getting old:

Stock Joke - *You know you're getting old when you suggest to an attractive former classmate at a reunion that you believe she was in your class, and she asks, "What did you teach?"*

Personalized - *For many years, I was known as the "Dick Clark" of Toastmasters, never seeming to age while many of my friends were wondering if there was even life after dinner. Then a terrible thing* *happened...Dick Clark had a stroke, I had several surgeries on my shoulder, and I started feeling less bulletproof.*

About that same time, I attended a 30th class reunion in Dallas. It was depressing. I hardly recognized anyone. There was, however, one very attractive lady who I did remember, so I walked over to her and said, "Hello, I'm Karl Righter. I believe you were in my class." She looked puzzled, then finally said, "What did you teach?"

By rewriting this generic joke, I turned it into a personal story that the audience could relate to. Note how much build-up I crafted in the *set-the-scene* step, using material which, in contrast to the joke, was true information about me. I actually was referred to for many years as the *Dick Clark* of Toastmasters. That set-up made the rewritten joke that followed seem more believable. I also added the funny line about *life after dinner*.

Longer Stories

It's not just one-liners that need to be rewritten and personalized. Longer stories may still seem out of place without some tailoring. My mentor Win Pendleton once saw a funny story in a book that he wanted to use. Here is how it appeared before he rewrote it:

A Baltimore newspaperman was invited to speak at a Chamber of Commerce meeting in a small Texas town. He was almost frightened to death when he noticed that most of the men in the audience were wearing six-shooters. His fears increased after he had finished speaking and sat down, because one of the men drew his guns and rushed toward the head table. "Don't be afraid of him," the president of the club said. "He's not going to bother you. He's after the man who invited you."

That story was potentially a great opening laugh-getter, but Win realized it wouldn't create a ripple if told as it was printed in the book. People no longer carry firearms to hear speakers, and he wasn't speaking in Texas either. So how was he to make that story fit his planned speech to a group of insurance salespeople in the auditorium of a schoolhouse in Effingham, Illinois? To begin with, he considered his audience and the place where he was to tell the story. He knew that his audience couldn't care less about a newspaperman from Baltimore whom they had never heard of. They came to hear Win, so he thought, "Why not rewrite this story and make me the butt of the joke?" Here's how he modified the story:

> *I hope this meeting tonight goes better than my last engagement. I was speaking to a group of Texas ranchers in a high school auditorium in Ft. Worth. This was the first time I had ever spoken in Texas and I was a little intimidated by these big, husky cowboys, some of whom were wearing pistols. But I had to make my speech, so I went ahead.*
>
> *After I had been talking for about two minutes, one of the men in the front row jumped up and yelled "Throw the bum out!" That's when I stopped and asked the president, "What's wrong? What did I say to offend that fellow?" The president replied, "Keep going. He's talking to the guy up here who invited you."*

Reruns

Many professional speakers have a favorite story that always produces a sure-fire laugh, and since they speak to many different audiences, they can keep using it from one engagement to the next. In most cases, however, the speaker will still need to tailor it to each event and audience. This is particularly true with *housekeeping humor,* which, as we learned in Chapter Two, *What's so funny?* is used in the opening minutes of a presentation to warm up the audience and establish common ground. Housekeeping humor typically references the hotel or venue, the food or service, the meeting arrangements, local news that is relevant to the event, your written introduction, or the event itself.

If you have had good results with a funny story and are scheduled to speak to a new group, you will probably want to use it again, but don't be fooled into thinking that just because something was funny before, that it will be funny again. You will more than likely need to adapt it to your new audience.

For example, I used to get a good laugh at the beginning of my keynote speech, *Laugh at Yourself, Others Are*, by telling a funny story about my daughter, Heather. The original idea for the gag came from a joke book one-liner about a father who disapproved of his daughter's boyfriend. To make it seem fresh and relevant, I had to alter it each time I used it to fit the occasion. Here is how I presented it in a speech to a local tourist industry association:

I am honored to be invited to speak to your organization. I wanted to invite my daughter Heather to this event as she is in the hospitality business, but she wanted to bring her boyfriend, and I am not real fond of the guy. This, of course distresses her, and she finally confronted me about it today. She said, "Dad, why don't you like Tom? How can you not like a guy who's doing 500 hours of community service?"

Each time I used that story, I would reframe Heather's interest in attending the event to match the purpose of the meeting or the demographics of the audience.

Make it Believable

As indicated, original humor is your best choice for entertaining your audience, but when you don't have the right personal story to make a point and get a laugh, you may achieve the same good results with canned humor that you rewrite and personalize. Make a point! Make them laugh! But make it believable!

(8)
Practice Makes Perfect

> *"For every finish-line tape a runner breaks --*
> *complete with the cheers of the crowd*
> *and the clicking of hundreds of cameras --*
> *there are the hours of hard and often lonely*
> *work that rarely gets talked about."*
>
> - Grete Waitz
> *Norwegian marathon runner*

How often have you spent days or weeks crafting and rehearsing a speech or presentation, and then on the night before you are to deliver it, you decide that it is pretty boring and needs some humor. So you hurriedly throw in a few jokes, hopefully on point, and then go to bed thinking you have a winner. Then the next day, you deliver your well-practiced speech in fine fashion, except for the two blown jokes that you failed to rehearse!

Using humor can be frightening enough when you are prepared, but when you don't practice your funny stories, the pressure to deliver mounts, your demeanor changes, and you may even have to read the joke (a killer of spontaneity). Consequently, if you struggle or fumble with the delivery of your humor, in contrast to your well-prepared talk, the audience may pick up on the fact that you are trying to be funny, thus ruining the element of surprise. But even worse, you may blow the punch line!

In my workshop, *Winning Your Audience With Bombproof Humor*, I reinforce the importance of practice by sharing the story of the minister who was preparing his sermon for Mother's Day:

> *Years ago, the minister at my church finally heeded the feedback of his elders, who had been criticizing him for his lackluster messages. He decided that the approaching Mothers' Day service with its larger-than-usual turnout would be the perfect time to introduce a new and more entertaining style. He found a funny quote in a reference book that he*

believed was perfect for the occasion: "Some of the happiest days of my life were spent in the arms of another man's wife...my mother!" This was indeed a clever line, but there were two problems with his decision: first, he did not practice the joke, and, second, he forgot to warn his wife that he was going to use it.

That Sunday morning, he was on a roll, blazing through his well-rehearsed sermon, when he came to that fateful place where he was to deliver his funny line. He began, "Some of the happiest days of my life were spent in the arms of another man's wife..." at which point he froze as he realized that the punch line was eluding him.

He glanced at his shocked wife sitting on the front row and panicked. He then quickly restarted the quote, thinking that the rest of it would come to him in the flow of telling it again, but it didn't!

By now his wife's shock had turned to rage, and the minister frantically made one more desperate attempt: "Some of the happiest days of my life were spent in the arms of another man's wife...(painful and pregnant pause) and for the life of me, I can't remember who it was!"

This story adheres to all of the rules of using *bombproof humor*: I didn't announce that I was about to tell a joke, I used a story that reinforced the point that practice is a critical success factor when delivering humor, and I made the humor believable by rewriting this joke as though it actually happened at our church. Plus, I have given it so many times, both in practice and in my workshops, that I can deliver it effortlessly and effectively. The laughter is almost always uproarious!

Practice Makes Perfect

It has been noted by coaches, teachers, and trainers that practice makes perfect. Repetition can truly help with becoming better at anything sports-related, and it's equally as important in public speaking. Just be sure to practice your humor as well. Have the punch line so well memorized that you can't possibly forget or fumble it.

As previously suggested, I also recommend trying out new humor on family and friends prior to attempting it before a live audience. Not only will the practice help you master the story, but you'll also find out whether it is perceived by others to be as funny as you think it is.

In reality, practice doesn't make perfect...perfect practice makes perfect! And much of practice comes with stage time...grabbing every opportunity to try new things and weed out humor that doesn't work.

(9)
Win Them Over Early

"The beginning is the most important part of the work."

- Plato

We often hear in speech courses or Toastmasters orientation that the first 30 seconds of a speech is critical to the success of your presentation. The implication is that if you can immediately pique the curiosity of your audience, ask a thought-provoking question, stir their imagination, or make them laugh, you have earned the right to ask for their undivided attention for at least a few more minutes, giving you precious time to establish your premise and objectives, and offer a potential payoff for the audience to stay the course.

While this concept is certainly sound, your game plan actually begins well before your first word is uttered. Here are some proven strategies to help you win over your audience early:

Event Promotion

When you are scheduled to speak to an association or group, you will often be asked for three things in advance: a synopsis of your speech, a personal bio, and an introduction for the master of ceremonies to use to introduce you. Each of these tools is an opportunity to build anticipation for your message before you even step up to the lectern!

Speech Synopsis - This overview of your presentation is typically used in printed newsletters, direct mail, web sites, or promotional e-mail announcements prior to the event to build anticipation for your presentation and boost attendance. In addition, it will often appear in the event's meeting agenda or conference program to continue promoting your part of the program. The synopsis should be brief, yet mention key points that will entice the association's members to attend and invite other guests. Here is the synopsis I provide to program organizers for my *Bombproof Humor* workshop:

Winning Your Audience With Bombproof Humor - Workshop Overview: Humor is the single most powerful card in the hand of the public speaker, meeting chairperson, or presenter. Humor breaks down communication barriers, warms up your audience, holds their attention, uplifts their spirits, and makes your message more memorable. In this concentrated workshop by humorist Karl Righter, attendees will learn fifteen ways humor can improve their presentations or speeches, dozens of types of humor and when to use them, five key steps to using bombproof humor, excellent sources for finding humorous material, proven methods of personalizing stock humor and making it sound genuine and believable, humor for special occasions, and much more!

Speaker Bio - This short personal bio is also used in printed newsletters, web sites, e-mail announcements, meeting agendas, or conference guides to establish you as an authority on your topic. It should avoid biographical information that does not support your agenda and instead should provide credentials relating to your particular topic. In keeping with the above example, here is the bio I provide for my *Bombproof Humor* workshop at Toastmasters conferences:

Winning Your Audience With Bombproof Humor - About the Presenter: The workshop presenter is acclaimed humorist and Past District Governor Karl Righter, DTM. Karl has been a professional speaker and corporate trainer for over 30 years, and is a frequent presenter at district, regional, and international Toastmasters conventions. He is a past winner of Toastmasters' highest humor competition, the Annual Humorous Speech Contest. His most frequently requested workshop by Toastmasters is "Winning Your Audience With Bombproof Humor."

Note that only the biographical information relevant to Toastmasters is used in this bio, as are my speaking credentials and references to the types of venues at which the workshop has been presented.

Speaker Introduction - Win Pendleton believed that this important document should be written word-for-word the way you want to be introduced. Don't send the program chairperson a long biography and expect him or her to extract the pertinent facts and write an introduction that will get you off to a dramatic start. This is *your* introduction. Give it to the program chairperson exactly as you want to be presented.

Providing a concise, prepared introduction in large type will simplify his or her responsibility, and your thoughtfulness will be appreciated. More important, you will be presented to the audience exactly as you require, heightening the anticipation. Plus, if you know exactly what the program chairperson is going to say, you can have a carefully rehearsed response, including a funny line, in your opening remarks, that will tie in with the introduction.

Provide enough background material to establish you as an authority on your subject. However, don't overdo it. If you are speaking to a group of IT representatives and you have a computer degree, by all means mention it. But don't overwhelm the audience with extraneous facts such as your association affiliations or the names and ages of your children, unless you can directly enhance your topic's appeal with this information.

Continuing with the previous examples, here is the written introduction for my *Bombproof Humor* workshop that I provide for the Toastmaster who will be introducing me:

Introduction for Karl Righter: Our workshop leader this morning is Past District 47 Governor Karl Righter, DTM. Karl has been a professional speaker and corporate trainer for over 30 years and has been a frequent presenter at a number of district, regional, and international Toastmasters conventions. His most frequently requested workshop by Toastmasters is the one he is giving this morning, "Winning Your Audience With Bombproof Humor." His humor column, "One Liners," has appeared in past issues of Toastmasters Magazine, and his "Righter's Top Ten" humor series has appeared periodically in the district newsletter and his two club newsletters for over 20 years. He is a past winner of Toastmasters' highest humor competition, the Annual Humorous Speech Contest. Please help me welcome our workshop leader for this morning, that forever-young gentleman known as the "Dick Clark" of Toastmasters, Karl Righter!

Note the similarities in wording to the promotional materials that preceded the event. Consistency is important when building a brand identity and awareness. The reference to Dick Clark was a set-up which allowed me to get my first laugh almost immediately as follows: "Thank you for that kind introduction. Last night, I was at the hospitality suite until after midnight, and right now, I'm feeling more like Dick Cheney than Dick Clark!"

These three items, the synopsis of your speech, your bio, and your written introduction, prepared with care and foresight exclusively by you, are instrumental in positioning you as an authority on your topic and building anticipation for your message before you even step to the lectern!

There's one other strategy that is important before you are introduced - mingling! Humorist Patricia Fripp is a great example of someone who warms up the audience by mingling before the meeting starts. Do you mix, mingle, and chat with the audience before your speech? If you socialize well, then when you are introduced, you already have plenty of friends in the audience.

Opening Strategies

Now that you've been introduced, you're ready to grab your audience by their collective collars. The first thirty seconds following your introduction can be the most critical part of your speech. During those few seconds, you have the complete attention of the audience. There is a natural air of expectancy in the room as you step to the lectern. Following are five effective techniques that you can employ to quickly capture the attention and imagination of your audience:

Thought-Provoking Question - The power of asking questions in your speeches is that it forces the audience to contemplate answers, thus drawing them into your presentation. Even better, opening your speech with a question draws the audience in at the most critical time of all when you are trying to connect with them and build anticipation for your message. Choose a question that generates curiosity for your theme or premise, or identifies a problem that needs to be solved. Here is the question I often open with in my entertaining keynote speech, *Laugh at Yourself, Others Are:*

What would you do if you found out that you have only six months to live? If your doctor said that in six months it would all be over, what would you change about your life? What would you do differently?

This is a thought-provoking question that sets up my speech's premise: *Life is short and we should really strive to enjoy the time we are given.* This question has the added benefit of also setting up an early humorous follow-up:

I've often pondered that question myself, and I've decided that if I ever have only six months to live, I'll move back to Buffalo, New York, because it will seem longer there!

Startling Statement - A powerful opening technique is the startling statement that jars the audience awake and builds anticipation for your message. It's a figurative slap in the face, a splash of cold water that momentarily rivets the audience. If the meeting room has a head table at which dignitaries are seated, I will often use a different opening in my keynote speech, *Laugh at Yourself, Others Are:*

Good evening. I read a shocking article in a recent issue of *Newsweek* which stated that in the United States today, one out of every three Americans suffers from moderate to severe emotional distress or depression.

This is a wake-up call for many in the audience who may be stressed or depressed, or know someone who is, and it will encourage them to stay tuned for a possible remedy. As with my thought-provoking six-months-to-live question described above, this opening has the added benefit of also setting up a humorous follow-up:

Think about that statistic: one out of three Americans suffers from moderate to severe emotional distress! If that is correct, then at least three people at this head table may be only weeks away from checking into the Betty Ford Clinic!"

This is a great one-two punch for opening a speech: a startling statement, followed by a laugh, this one at the expense of those seated at the head table.

You are now off and running with your audience fully on board. Be sure to keep the momentum going by using *bombproof humor* throughout your presentation.

Opening Joke - In the first two types of speech openings just described, the *thought-provoking question* and *the startling statement,* I crafted the examples in a way that set up add-on humorous tag lines. A stand-alone opening joke also works just as well to warm up your audience. One commonly used type, *housekeeping humor,* was described in Chapter Two. As you may recall, this type of comedy is used in the opening minutes of a presentation to warm up the audience and establish common ground. The following is an example of an opening joke I use sometimes when I speak to a small association. It references the written introduction used to present me to the audience:

> *Thank you for that kind introduction. That was certainly much better than the one I received recently at a Rotary Club luncheon. The program chairperson read my bio as provided, then added, "I've heard Karl Righter speak, and I've heard him eat. Personally, I'd rather hear him speak."*

Although this is clearly a one-liner, it fits the profile of *bombproof humor* as it unfolds smoothly and seems like a true personal experience, making the punch line an effective surprise. It establishes common ground with the audience as virtually every event features a speaker introduction. Also, by poking fun at myself, I put the audience at ease and let them know I don't take myself too seriously. I've thus begun my speech with a tension-releasing laugh that bonds my audience to me.

Professional speaker Win Pendleton was from the small town of Windermere, Florida. He loved to open his speeches with *small-town humor.* Here is one of his funniest openers:

> *Your MC mentioned that I'm from the small town of Windermere. It's basically a boring place, but occasionally we do have some excitement. Last summer the packing house burned down. It caught fire about*

nine o'clock at night. Ordinarily it would have burned down in about an hour, but we have a volunteer fire department, and they arrived in about ten minutes. Those guys are good! They were able to keep that fire going until three o'clock in the morning!

The challenge with this type of opening is finding a smooth segue from the joke into your main speech. Here is how Win followed the above small-town story:

Whether you are from a small town as I am or from one of the great cities of America, you cannot help but be concerned about the problems we all face with...(and so on into his speech).

I have sometimes used the following opening joke when giving my humorous keynote address, *Laugh at Yourself, Others Are*. When I use this particular opening, I provide a written introduction for the program chairperson's use with these closing words: "It warms the cockles of my heart to present at this time a very funny speaker, Karl Righter!" My opening laugh comes immediately when I acknowledge the introduction as follows:

Thank you Mr. Chairman. I'm relieved that you won't have to sit there all evening with cold cockles.

As previously indicated, *housekeeping humor* can also reference the meeting venue. When I spoke at the Toastmasters International Convention in Miami Beach in 2000, I used this opener that I borrowed from Win Pendleton:

This is the first time I have been in one of these fancy Miami Beach hotels, and I wanted to be sure and tip the bellman properly, so I asked him, "What is the average tip here in Miami Beach?" He said, "Twenty-five dollars."

I didn't want to seem cheap so I gave him the twenty-five dollars. But I said to him, "If twenty-five dollars is the average tip here, you must be getting rich." "No, sir!" he replied. "In all the time I've worked here, this is the first average tip I've ever received!"

Humorous Personal Story - The next type of opener is the personal story. We've previously discussed the power of these introspective narratives that humanize you and connect you with the audience. People love stories, and the right ones add a powerful dimension to your speech. When you open your talk with the right humorous story, you immediately bond with the audience on a personal level and set the tone for a warm, entertaining speech.

In a contest speech entitled *When The Student is Ready,* a talk about the importance of role models, I opened with this personal story:

It was a beautiful, crisp fall Saturday morning. I had been up for hours when my daughter Heather came shuffling into the kitchen... yawning, and rubbing her eyes, trying to wake up. I said, "Good morning, sleepyhead! You've missed the best part of the day! I've already run six miles and cleaned out the garage!"

She looked at me in utter disbelief and said, "So what's next, a root canal? At least when I have a day off from school, I can tell the difference!"

I started to say something smart, but I bit my lip, because I knew she was right! In fact, I was such a workaholic that once when my wife said to me, "Karl, you really need to stop and smell the roses," my first reaction was to try to delegate that chore to Heather! Of course, children don't have to be told to stop and smell the roses. That's what they do best! It is we adults who have somewhere along the way lost that childlike enthusiasm for life!

This opening story contains a couple laughs while establishing the premise for my speech about role models. Everyone has stories like this. Our lives are rich with these kinds of moments, many of which bring laughter along with them. Write them down when they occur. They are effective ways to open your speech and relate to your audience.

Teasing the Celebrities - You will notice that most of the preceding openers involved self-deprecating humor. Audiences enjoy this kind of humor because it is non-threatening and positions you as someone who can take a joke. However, another category of laugh-getting openers includes quips told on the celebrities present at the event. An example of this type of opening was included previously in the section describing the *Startling Statement* opening. However, it was a non-specific example in that it targeted those seated at the head table rather than a particular person.

In general, there is nothing wrong with teasing the person who introduces you, or the president of the club, the program chairperson, or any other prominent member of the host organization. However, the person should be well-known and well-liked, and able to take a joke, or else your humor may misfire. Find out in advance who is the one person in the organization that everybody loves. That's the one you can usually kid.

It's also not a bad idea to seek permission from your intended target to humorously include that person in your opening remarks. Nevertheless, if the person is the president of the club, it is safe to assume that the audience knows and likes that person or he or she wouldn't be president.

A good strategy when employing this humor is to show the audience that you can "take it" by telling a story or two on yourself. Then you can slip in a humorous reference to someone at the head table who is in full view of the entire audience. Here is an example of a celebrity jab I used at an officer installation:

> *Thank you, Mr. President, for that kind introduction. Ladies and Gentlemen, in a few minutes I will be discharging John from office, but this is not a reason to be sad. You are not losing your president, you are gaining a parking space!*

Use Your Imagination

The previous strategies are five effective techniques to open your speeches with humor. There are many other attention-getting starters such as a humorous gesture or pratfall, a challenge to the audience, a couple lines of a popular song either sung or recited, a magic trick, a famous quote, or any of the other types of humor described in Chapter Two.

One of the greatest openings in Toastmasters World Championship history involved a pratfall of epic proportions. In his 2001 winning contest speech, *Ouch*, Darren LaCroix walked out onto the stage in front of 2,000 people in the audience, paused, and said...

Can you remember a moment when a brilliant idea flashed into your head? It was perfect for you...then, all of a sudden, from the depths of your brain, another thought forced its way through the enthusiasm until finally it shouted...

YEAH, great idea, but...(Darren then falls face-forward onto the stage) ...what if you fall on your face? (audience laughs)

(still face down and speaking into his lapel microphone) What do you do when you *fall on your face? Do you try to jump right up and hope no one noticed? (audience laughs) Are you more concerned with what other people will think than what you can learn from this?*

Mr. Contest Chair...friends, and people way in the back...(Darren then leaps to his feet)...OUCH! Did you feel I stayed down too long? Have YOU ever...stayed down...too long?

When Darren acknowledged the Contest Chair while he was still face down on the stage, he generated one of the loudest, longest laughs I have ever heard in any contest! Darren took a risk by doing something completely off the wall (and on the floor), and it paid huge dividends with a world championship! Based upon the electric response to his pratfall, Darren says he knew he had the trophy at that point!

Use your imagination. Pay attention to how other speakers open their talks. For example, Anthony Robbins has high-energy music playing before his audience even enters the meeting room. Imagine waiting in the hall for the doors to open and hearing pulse-pounding music originating from behind the closed doors. It's definitely an excitement builder and gets the audience's adrenaline going.

Remember, your objective is to make your event, and the first moments of your speech, captivating, thought-provoking, and entertaining. Grab your audience right from the start and don't let them go.

(10)
Leave Them Laughing

"A speech is like a love affair. Any fool can start it, but to end it requires considerable skill."

- Lord Mansfield

It is always a speaker's fervent hope that the person who introduces him or her gives a spirited and enthusiastic introduction that generates hearty applause and anticipation for the speech. As previously suggested, you play an important role in that by providing the master of ceremonies with the introduction you want to receive. Once you have been presented to your audience and the curtain raised, however, you are on your own.

You will feel even more alone when you get to your conclusion. There will be no gracious and eager MC standing by who will pave the way for your stirring, dramatic conclusion. Closing a speech is a do-it-yourself proposition, and too often, we don't do it very well.

Sometimes we'll *circle the airport* several times, hoping to discover a clear-cut path to touchdown, until we finally offer a weak "thank you" and sit down. Or we may run out of gas and barely limp in, drawing no real conclusions to our topic or offering a strong call to action. Other times, not knowing how to land, we sputter and repeat ourselves.

I heard a story about one speaker who droned on so long at an event that only one person remained in the audience when he finally stopped. He sheepishly went over and thanked the person for staying until the end of his talk. The lone survivor replied, "Don't thank me, I'm the next speaker!"

The Best Way to End Your Speech

My mentor Win Pendleton once told me, "Karl, there is only one truly memorable way to bring down the curtain - and that is with humor! If you want people to remember you and what you said, the old vaudeville rule *always leave them laughing* still holds true. There is no sweeter sound to a speaker's ears than the sound of applause *and* laughter as you depart the lectern!"

A funny wrap-up to your speech offers definitive evidence that you are comfortable, in control, and that you have finished. Adds Win, "You tell your funny concluding story, and as the laughter rises from the audience, you step back, bow, and allow the laughter to blend with the applause. You can't have a better send-off than that."

As covered in Chapter One, a hilarious close accomplishes a number of other objectives as well:

Ends Your Speech on an Upbeat Note - When your call-to-action incorporates humor, the impact of your closing message is enhanced. You will leave your audience in a positive frame of mind. They will remember having had an enjoyable experience, and they will be more inclined to embrace your point of view.

Creates Ongoing Goodwill - The entertaining speaker will be the one that is remembered, and recommended! A great speaker does more than make a speech...a great speaker makes a difference! And humor can make a great speech even better!

It has been said that the two most critical parts of a speech are the opening and the conclusion. Use your two funniest stories, the second funniest one in the opening to hook them early, and your best one at the end to leave them laughing!

Start strong, finish stronger!

Examples of Humorous Closers

In my keynote speech, *Laugh at Yourself, Others Are,* I talk about the importance of maintaining a sense of humor during life's challenging times. It is peppered with funny stories and quips illustrating how to see the humor in almost any situation. To reinforce these messages in my conclusion and leave the audience laughing, I end with the following humorous poem:

> *It is easy enough to be pleasant*
> *When life is all carefree and chipper,*
> *But the person worthwhile*
> *Is the one who can smile,*
> *When their tie gets caught in their zipper.*

In my contest speech, *The Music Within,* I talked about the importance of discovering our individual gifts and talents, and not letting our music die inside. Sprinkled throughout were references to country music and my professional piano playing. I concluded the speech with the following observation and song parody:

> *We all have music within us...a special gift or talent waiting to be discovered and unlocked. My gift has always been my music, but it took years to fully embrace its diversity. I used to laugh at the slapstick nature of many country songs. Now, I've learned to appreciate the deeper meanings of the words. As I leave you tonight, I hope that you will invite me to visit with you again, but if it is not to be, I'll reflect upon the words of my favorite country song, "If That Phone Don't Ring, I'll Know It's You!"*

In my contest speech for a past humorous speech contest, I crafted a talk about the challenges of getting old. It was entitled *I'm Not Bulletproof Anymore.* Instead of one funny closing line, I wrapped three gags, including a quote, into my tightly woven conclusion:

> *Humorist Roy Hatten once said, "Don't take yourself too seriously. The size of your funeral will largely depend upon whether or not it rains that day!" With that being said, I have specified in my will that I want the cheapest funeral available, because no one is going to profit from my death! I want the Discount Funeral Special. That's where they put you in the trunk of your car and leave you in a tow-away zone!*

Fellow Toastmasters, In closing, I admit that I'm not bulletproof any more. I know we can't stay young forever, but I've found that we can be immature for the rest of our lives!

When you are the keynote speaker on a program that has run long, this tale of two young lovers is a great way to end your speech and leave a pleasant taste in people's mouths while showing them that you are quite aware of the time:

I've enjoyed our time together this evening, but I feel like my neighbor's son Chris who was recently walking through the Mall with his girlfriend. At some point he stopped, put his arm around her and said, "Kerry, I love you. Will you marry me?" She was thrilled and said, "Oh, yes, I'll marry you." My neighbor said they continued to walk for quite awhile with neither one of them saying anything more. Apparently after an hour of complete silence, Kerry turned to her boyfriend and said, "Chris, why don't you say something?" He replied, "It seems to me that I've probably said too much as it is." Ladies and gentlemen, I believe I may have as well. So I bid you a good evening, and I thank you for the honor of being your speaker at this special event.

In a speech about the importance of a positive attitude entitled *The Glass Half Full*, I close with this funny quip:

All good things come to an end. Speeches should also! I have been encouraging you not to ever lose your sense of humor! A positive attitude can help you deal with life's inevitable setbacks, even a terminal illness! The widow next door told me recently that her doctor had given her only six months to live! I said, "What are you going to do?" "I told him I couldn't pay him," she replied, "and he gave me another six months!" Ladies and gentlemen, I hope to see all of you again, and I hope that I won't have to wait another six months!

Note that all of the previous examples do more than just end their respective speeches on an upbeat note. They all make a concluding point or restate the premise of the talk in an entertaining way, and they all employ *bombproof humor* techniques. What better way to end your fine speech!

   Remember, always leave them laughing and you will be remembered as an entertaining speaker.

(11)
Avoiding the Pratfalls of Speaking

"An ounce of prevention is worth a pound of cure."

- Benjamin Franklin

According to Webster's dictionary, a pratfall is a humiliating mistake or blunder. Public speaking and delivering effective humor are loaded with potential pratfalls of which you should be aware and avoid.

This chapter deals with the more common ones and how to avoid them. When prevention isn't possible, we'll also cover how to respond to the unavoidable gaffes and get a laugh in the process.

Types of Humor to Avoid

Lengthy Jokes - A joke that takes too long to develop may call attention to itself, thus costing you the element of surprise. It probably doesn't add much value to your message either. The exception is when you share a humorous story to reinforce an important point. As we've indicated, a story that adds value to your speech stands on its own merits whether it generates a laugh or not.

How do you know if your joke is taking too long to deliver? There are signs. People yawning is the first sign. People looking at their watches is the second sign. People banging their watches on the table to get them to run faster is a major tipoff!

Off-Color Stories - There is way too much clean humor in the world to resort to blue or off-color material. If you can't tell your joke in church, leave it out!

Defects/Put-Down Humor - This type of humor pokes fun at an individual's shortcomings or defects, and can be embarrassing to the person who is the target of the joke. For example, if the president of the association to whom you are speaking is short, he has probably heard every *short* joke there is. Why humiliate him in front of his peers? Don't go there.

Ethnic/Sexist Jokes - Dean Martin was famous for his celebrity roasts, and is particularly remembered for his classic sexist joke at the expense of Angie Dickinson: "She's no dumb blonde...I've seen her roots!" As funny as that might be in a roast, it is inappropriate at most other events. Why risk offending even a single individual with a sexist or ethnic joke. Note that defects, ethnic, sexist, and put-down humor can almost always be rewritten and told on yourself, making it non-threatening to the audience. Self-directed humor is the most effective humor there is, because we like to laugh at others, not at ourselves! Audiences love a speaker who can kid himself or herself, so why not get in on all the fun!

Puns - Puns are often referred to as the lowest form of comedy. They frequently elicit groans from the audience. Unless you have a blockbuster of a pun, skip this type of humor as it is certainly not bombproof.

Inside Jokes - An inside joke is one that a majority of the audience is not privy to, and thus will elicit few laughs. For example, if you shared a funny exchange with an officer of the association prior to the meeting, it may lose a lot in the translation an hour later. Make sure the audience understands the context of the humor, or you will draw blank stares.

Politically Incorrect - According to Wikipedia, the term *politically incorrect* connotes language, ideas, and behavior unconstrained by concerns about offending or expressing bias regarding various groups of people. This may include social, institutional, occupational, gender, racial, cultural, sexual orientation, disability, and age-related contexts, or humor about body parts and body functions. This type of humor could offend a large portion of your audience, so why risk it.

Dialects - Doing a dead-on impersonation of the movie character Forest Gump can be quite entertaining, but if you aren't very good at dialects, you end up looking silly. Try out your impersonations on friends and family first to see if they are well-received.

The Written Joke - Reading a joke can be counterproductive in that you lose the spontaneity and connection with the audience. Suddenly you are out of your rhythm, and the timing which is so important to delivering *bombproof humor* is sacrificed. One of the rules of *bombproof humor* is practice. Practice leads to smoother delivery and better dramatic effect. Win Pendleton wrote, "If you have to read your story, you have failed to follow the basic rule of being funny - you don't know your story. Never use a story in your speech that you don't know well enough to tell from memory."

The Apology - *Bombproof humor* means never having to say you're sorry, or explain a failed joke. That's because *bombproof humor* adds value regardless of the laughter it generates. It's also not advised to laugh at your own jokes. That is the same thing as applauding yourself. Still, laughter is contagious. Maybe you *can* start a wave by cracking *yourself* up!

Turn Disaster into Laughter

No matter how well-prepared and rehearsed you are, mishaps occasionally occur during a speech. Someone in the audience falls out of their chair. A person knocks over a glass of iced tea reaching for the butter. A waiter clearing tables drops a tray of dishes. You inadvertently blind yourself with your own power point presentation. You toss Hershey's Kisses into your audience for a Valentine's Day speech and have some splash down in hot coffee. You walk into the audience with the microphone and pull the entire lectern to the floor.

Such pratfalls may ruin your momentum unless you can turn them to humorous advantage. You may not be able to anticipate every possible fiasco, but it is a good idea to have rehearsed a few snappy comebacks for some of the more common setbacks of speaking. Especially effective are ones that incorporate self-deprecating humor, as they endear you to your audience and let them know you are unflappable and can handle disaster. Here are some examples of snappy comebacks for a variety of situations:

Dishes crash to the floor: "Clean up, aisle four!"

Microphone squeals: "Sound system by Mattel"

You fall on your face on the way to the lectern: "I will now take questions from the floor."

Flopping microphone: "Housekeeping! There's a loose nut on the microphone!"

In response to a heckler in audience: "Security, table six. Security, table six."

The bulb burns out on your projector: "Power Point seemed like such a bright idea at the time!"

You fall through a rotten floorboard on an elevated platform: "Don't mind me. It's just a stage I'm going through."

When a cell phone goes off in audience, you pretend to answer on your cell phone: "Hi Honey! Yeah. I'll get a gallon of milk on the way home." *Another good response:* "Hold my calls!"

A member of the audience is heard snoring: "Well, I guess I won't get a referral from him!"

Minimal applause: "Hold your applause...oh wait, you did!"

Lackluster Applause

Speaking of applause, the amount you receive after an introduction is often a factor of how enthusiastically you are presented by the toastmaster or program chairperson. A lukewarm reading of your prepared introduction could lead to a lackluster round of applause.

Your audience may also be feeling sluggish after a heavy steak dinner. When the silence is deafening, and you are addressing an otherwise friendly or playful audience, you may want to consider one of these snappy openers:

I should warn you that the same person who wrote that scintillating intro also wrote my speech.

I don't get it. It says right here in my notes - pause for applause.

I've always heard that applause works better when you use both hands!

Thanks for that rousing round of indifference, but I can get that at home.

Dealing with Hecklers

Into the life of every speaker eventually comes a heckler. The best approach is to ignore the individual until he or she starts annoying the audience as well as you. Once the audience is on your side, you can use your mastery of humor to embarrass that person into backing off. After they realize that the audience is laughing at *them* and is not in agreement with their heckling, they will usually stop.

In his humor boot camp, Darren LaCroix relates the story of a stand-up comedian who was being unmercifully heckled by an old lady in a wheelchair. Finally, when nothing else worked, he walked down from the stage and wheeled her out of the room to thunderous laughter and applause. It occurred to me when I heard this story that the only thing that would have been funnier is if, when the comedian returned to the stage, he had said, "I wish all hecklers came with wheels."

Another approach to stopping a relentless heckler is to take a vote! Again, ignore the person until you are certain that they are also annoying the audience. Then stop your presentation and say, "OK folks, let's vote the heckler off the island. How many think he should leave here and go annoy his wife?" The vote will probably be unanimous.

Losing your Place

If you speak often enough, there will come a time when you momentarily lose your place or train of thought. If the gaffe is obvious, you may want to recover with a well-timed quip. Here are several snappy, self-deprecating comebacks you can use when you lose your place during your speech:

I pause to ask myself a question – where the heck am I?

He who hesitates is lost.

Ooops! My teleprompter just shorted out. Go ahead without me!

I guess I carried that pregnant pause to full term.

Of all the things I've ever lost, I miss my next thought the most!

They say your memory is the second thing to go. I guess the first thing you lose is your place.

I feel like the bug that hit the windshield of your car. I can still see you, but I'm not getting through to you.

If any of you need to go to the bathroom, now is a good time.

This is not a senior moment - it is a leave of absence!

Disclaimers

Sometimes you can diffuse a possible negative situation with a humorous disclaimer early in your presentation. Here are a few examples:

Note: the following question-and-answer session may provoke anxiety, profuse sweating, and meaningless babble by the presenter.

Before we begin, here are the odds for tonight's meeting: winning the 50-50 drawing...one chance in 25, fully digesting your Black & Decker Road-Kill Almondine entreé...one chance in thirty.

Before I begin my keynote address, please consider the Surgeon General's warning that suppressing laughter may cause painful gas.

I have been asked by the hotel to read a disclaimer before I begin: Warning: the following speech may cause drowsiness. Do not attempt to use sharp utensils if impaired.

Question-and-Answer Sessions

A great opportunity for humor is during question-and-answer sessions. If you have a standard presentation, then after awhile, you can anticipate the most frequently asked questions and have humorous answers ready and rehearsed.

During the Q&A of my *Bombproof Humor* workshop, I am often asked if it is OK to laugh at your own jokes. My reply: "Yes, but you run the risk of being the only one laughing!"

Having a humorous answer can also diffuse a tense situation. During the presidential debates between Reagan and Mondale, Reagan anticipated that he would get a question about his age. Sure enough, he was asked if the age issue was going to be a problem. He confidently replied, "I want you to know that I will not make age an issue of this campaign. I am not going to exploit for political purposes my opponent's youth and inexperience."

But What if You do Bomb?

If you faithfully follow the *bombproof humor* strategy, you won't need snappy comebacks to bail you out of a bad joke. But sometimes you are put on the spot at a gathering when asked to tell a funny story, so you may need a few ready-made quips should you fall short of a full belly laugh. Humorist John Kinde believes that, "With the security blanket of a good saver, you feel free to take bigger risks since you have a funny line to back it up. That gives you more confidence."

Here are a few good retorts for when your joke bombs:

This microphone seems to be picking up the punch lines but not the laughs.

Wow! Without the laughter, it looks like I'm going to finish way ahead of schedule!

If you think I'm too serious now, wait until I drop the humor!

Hey, it's a lot easier to get a new audience than a new joke!

Try to laugh all at once, not sequentially!

Some day you'll look back at that and laugh! Too bad it wasn't today!

Hey, where were you last week when I was trying to be serious?

Normally you should avoid snappy come-backs that imply that the audience is not smart enough to get the humor. However, if you have been prodded into telling a joke by the audience, and you have a good rapport with them, you can take the gloves off!

Sometimes during the question and answer period of a presentation, I will get a tough question. If I need to stall for a moment to gather my thoughts, I will often say, "That's a good question! Of course, whenever a speaker says, *that's a good question*, it usually means it's a lot better question than the answer's going to be!"

To summarize, when you bomb, there are three things you should do: 1) have several snappy comebacks ready for such a situation, 2) learn from the experience and make the story better, or replace it with a better gag for next time, and 3) don't tell the audience you read my book! (Ah Ha! Did you recognize that rule-of-three joke?)

The Bottom Line

The entertaining speaker should always be prepared, not only with his or her speech, but by being ready for any contingency. The most important thing to remember: don't lose your sense of humor when things don't go as planned. Your audience will pick up on your angst and feel uncomfortable if you do. Have the last laugh when good props go bad, or after other assorted pratfalls. Your audience will love you for it!

A highly rated book on recovering from speaking disasters and challenges is *What to Say When You're Dying on the Platform* by Lilly Walters. Check it out.

(12)
Where's the Humor?

"Humor is everywhere, in that there's irony in just about anything a human does."

Bill Nye
Comedian

Humor is everywhere, and it has the potential to brighten our day and lift our spirits, but usually we don't notice it because we are too preoccupied with our own problems and responsibilities. As speakers, the more we study humor, the better we will become at recognizing it when it surfaces, especially if we can see the humor in our own uncomfortable or embarrassing situations. 1999 World Champion Craig Valentine says, "Don't add humor to a speech...uncover the humor opportunities already there!" This is how Hollywood makes movies! They look at real life and strip away all the boring parts! But where do we find the humor for our presentations when life doesn't just hand it to us?

Be a Student

Humorist Charles Jarvis was a dentist in San Marcos, Texas, when he was asked to speak at a Rotary Club years ago. He shared a few of the funny things that happen in dental offices, such as patients asking if they had to floss *all* of their teeth! "Just the ones you want to keep," was his answer. People laughed, and Jarvis was so invigorated by the response that he made the decision to become a humorous keynote speaker. For the next five years, he got up every morning at 5 a.m. and studied the theory of comedy. In doing so, he developed the ability to see the funny side of virtually everything life had to offer, and he ultimately became one of America's funniest professional speakers. He was a student first, and then a success.

You may not wish to become a humorous keynote speaker, but you surely want to be entertaining when you do make a speech or presentation. Consequently, you need to become a student of humor. You may need to reference this book often to pick up many of the nuances of comedy. There are also many other great resources for humor which we will discuss in this chapter.

Choose Your Environment

One of the smartest decisions you can make is to hang around funny people, and minimize your exposure to the toxic ones in your life.

A good source of funny people is Toastmasters International, as this is an organization that encourages the development of good communication skills that include the use of humor. As such, Toastmasters often attracts individuals who already have a good sense of humor, or at least like to laugh, and by surrounding yourself with these kinds of upbeat people, their enthusiasm, techniques, and positive attitude will likely rub off on you.

Members also receive a monthly publication called *Toastmaster Magazine*, which often contains excellent articles on how to use humor. Twice a year, members have the opportunity to attend a Toastmasters district conference, plus the Annual International Convention, where educational workshops often feature humor themes.

As a new Toastmaster, you will also be assigned a more experienced member as a mentor. Ask for a mentor who is regarded as a humorous speaker in the club and commit to learning from that person, just as I learned at the feet of Win Pendleton.

Enter every speech contest that you can, especially the Annual Humorous Speech Contest. Competition makes you better. Stage time! Stage time! Stage time!

Finding Humor

So where do you find good humor? It's everywhere, if you know where to look. Here are a few sources:

Observational Humor - Humorist John Kinde notes the difficulty of finding humor that appeals to diverse audiences: "A group is more likely to laugh at humor with which the majority of people can identify. This is why an audience of both young and old people may pose a challenge. Why a group of mixed cultures may pose a challenge. Why a group of men and women can pose a challenge."

Fortunately, these challenges can be mitigated using observational humor. At a typical meeting, several funny things may occur during the course of the program prior to you being introduced as the speaker. Jotting down a note or two when this happens (*observational humor*) provides an opportunity to interject some spontaneous levity into your speech to which the entire audience will relate. Says Kinde, "The whole group has the common experience of seeing and hearing the same things that triggered the creation of the humor in your mind. They all heard the false fire alarm go off during the previous speaker's talk. They all heard the president of the organization forget the vice president's name. They all ate the same meal with the cold soup before you were introduced to speak. This is also why current-event humor can sometimes work. If it's in the news, it's probably part of the common experience."

Personal Experiences - Keep a humor journal - a notebook in which you jot down everything that makes you laugh during the day. As we previously stated, personal stories are best for connecting with the audience because they are authentic, not canned. They are believable, and they provide the opportunity to poke fun at yourself - always a big hit! By religiously writing down these funny situations, you will create a treasure trove of original humor.

The Internet - I have become a big fan of the Internet when I need on-target humor. For example, I recently needed a funny line about police officers, so I googled *police humor* and up came 2.7 million hits! Of course, with such an obscene amount of options, I was able to find exactly what I needed. Two other great web sites which are loaded with material and resources are *www.laugh.com* and *www.comedy.com*. Humorist John Kinde, frequently quoted in this book, has a great web site and newsletter for studying humor at *www.humorpower.com*.

Quotes - Many quotes are funny. For example, Oscar Wilde once said, "The proper basis for marriage is mutual misunderstanding." Use a quote to make a point in your speech. Use a funny quote to also entertain your audience! Once again, you can use the Internet to find a quote on virtually any topic. As an example, if you google *funny political quotes,* you pull up over 750,000 ideas, including this gem from a former U.S. president: "It is clear our nation is reliant upon big foreign oil. More and more of our imports come from overseas."

Local Comedy Clubs - You can learn a lot by observing the professionals. Of course, stand-up comedy is not bombproof because the audience is expecting one laugh after another, but you can certainly pick up some good material while also observing how the comedian interacts with the audience.

Movies - A good comedy can provide ideas for humorous stories or one-liners. In the theater, it's tough to take notes, but renting the DVD provides an opportunity to periodically stop the movie and write down the things that make you laugh.

Books & CDs - Being an avid student means reading books, and listening to tapes and CDs in the car, so while we're on the subject of the Internet, go to *www.amazon.com* and initiate a search for *humor books.* You will find that there are over 70,000 to choose from, each with a peer-review rating that helps you determine how helpful the book has been for others. A few of my favorites:

2100 Laughs for All Occasions by Robert Orben
Milton Berle's Private Joke File by Milton Berle
Nothing But Winners by Pat Williams and Ken Hussar
Comedy Writing Secrets by Melvin Helitzer
Jay Leno's Headlines by Jay Leno
Stand-Up Comedy: The Book by Judy Carter
David Letterman's Book of Top Ten Lists by David Letterman
We're Roasting Harry Tuesday Night by Ed McManus and Bill Nicholas

Comics - Some of my funniest lines have been inspired by the daily comic strips: workplace humor from *Dilbert,* relationship humor from *The Middletons* and *Blondie,* humor about children from *Calvin & Hobbes,* military humor from *Beetle Bailey,* humor about deadbeats from *Andy Capp, etc.* Most comic strips feature short, snappy quips or one-liners that you can incorporate into your speeches. And *www.comics.com* gives you access to hundreds of strips and editorial cartoons not carried by your local newspaper. A funny cartoon can also add visual levity to a Power Point presentation.

Radio & Television - I love the Comedy Channel on cable TV. On Sirius satellite radio in my car, I listen to the comedy stations. Old TV shows like *I Love Lucy*, *Seinfeld*, and *Roseanne* are classics. I think these shows are funnier than many of today's sitcoms, and the humor is less likely to be in mainstream consciousness and so will seem more original and fresh.

Remember, rewrite stock humor to personalize it whenever possible. The put-down humor that is characteristic of shows like *Roseanne* and other sitcoms is great for celebrity roasts and self-directed humor. I encourage you to carry a digital recorder with you in the car to record humor that you hear on the radio while driving.

Even commercials offer opportunities for finding humor. Comedian Mike Williams was amused by a commercial for Ex-Lax in which the talking head claimed, "Ex-Lax...it works while you sleep!" During a show, comedian Bill Engvall relayed a funny Jimmy Dean commercial as follows: "The eggs are from real chickens, the milk is from real cows, and the sausage is from Jimmy Dean!" And, DeBeers, the diamond company, gets points for unintentional humor with its slogans. Originally their tag line was, "A diamond is forever." Then they changed it to, "Diamonds...take her breath away." Then I heard the clincher, "Diamonds...render her speechless." That's when I thought to myself, why don't they just say it - "Diamonds...that will shut her up!"

Bumper Stickers & Greeting Cards - There is humor everywhere, and greeting cards, bumper stickers, and T-shirts are a reliable source of funny lines. I thought this was a creative bumper sticker when I saw it: *Make something idiot-proof and a better idiot will buy it.* I also recently saw a couple standing next to each other at the mall wearing really clever T-shirts. His shirt said in big, bold letters, *NOTHING*, and her shirt said, *NEXT TO NOTHING*.

Mistakes Can be Funny - By now we know that SpellCheck is not infallible. For example, *if you halve a computer, and it has SpellCheck, it wood seam that this is awl ewe really knead to right correctly.* Obviously what's correct can be hilariously wrong, as with the previous sentence of correctly spelled words. Here are some funny examples of SpellCheck errors from the American Bar Association:

A legal secretary who didn't know a proper name used "Dear Sir or Madam," but the autotext feature found nothing wrong with her misspelled word in "Dear Sir or Madman."

SpellCheck suggested changing a first name of Myron to "moron."

SpellCheck didn't challenge "incontinence" instead of "inconvenience" as in: "We sincerely apologize for any incontinence caused by our delay."

SpellCheck kept trying to turn a person's name "Trish" into "trash."

In the early days of voice-recognition software, a program had faithfully replaced the dictated "Alzheimer's disease" with "old-timer's disease" throughout the report. This malapropism has since become part of mainstream culture.

When "does not" was typed "doe snot," SpellCheck let it through without question, perhaps because the error was made during deer-hunting season.

Involving the Audience - Many people love to be involved in the speaker's presentation. Most of us are hams and love the attention, and the audience really gets into it as well. For example, I usually open my *Bombproof Humor* workshop with an audience task: I have everyone stand, turn to the person next to them, and tell their favorite joke. This fills the room with laughter and gets the workshop off to a riotous start. I then ask for a volunteer to repeat a really funny joke he or she heard or told. I have gained some great humor for my archives this way. And the volunteer is rewarded with a prize for participating.

Writing Original Humor

As we have said, the best humor is that which is drawn from personal experiences. Such stories are authentic, believable, and practically write themselves if you relate them essentially as they occurred to you in real life.

Most entertaining speakers and humorists are also adept at creating their own humor from scratch. Although a complete thesis on how to write original humor is beyond the scope of this book, here are some simple templates you can experiment with:

Rule of Three - As discussed in Chapter Two, *What's so Funny?*, the rule of three in humor is an effective humor style. Essentially you have a three-part story: the first two parts of the humorous story set the tone and direction, like the train going down the track, and the third part, the punch line (or train wreck), throws a curve and provides the element of surprise.

Practice creating your own rule-of-three jokes, one of the easiest humor styles to learn. Select a theme, such as your first car - let's say it was a Volkswagen Beetle. List ten things you liked about your car, then select the two best items for your two-part set-up. Then list ten strange or negative things about the car and select the one item that most strongly contrasts with the first two items. The end result might look something like this: "I loved my Beetle! It was easy to park, got great gas mileage, and it had a spare tire under the hood!"

Exaggeration - This is an easy technique to learn because we all exaggerate or embellish our words or stories from time to time in social situations. As a humor style, you simply take this practice to an extreme point of view.

Example: "My teenage son is on a life support system...the refrigerator!" Similarly, I once referred to the high concessionary prices at the airport in this way: "What's with the prices of food and drinks at the airport? Do these people live in the real world? I had a cup of coffee prior to boarding my flight recently...$165!"

As an exercise, write down a key point that you wish to make in your presentation. Decide what your intent is going to be when you make that point. Then consider ways that you could use exaggeration to really emphasize that point or get a laugh.

In my humorous speech entitled *I'm Not Bulletproof Anymore*, I used exaggeration to squeeze laughs out of the distress associated with getting old. My intent was to convey that we need to be able to laugh at ourselves. So I went through the process of writing down as many old-age scenarios as I could think of. In this original list were phrases like *senior moments, driving slowly, false teeth, the good old days, birthday cakes, hearing aids, Geritol, choice of clothing,* etc. I then looked at each item and analyzed how I could exaggerate that expression. What I came up with were some dramatic ways of taking these points to higher levels. At the end of the process, these were the three funniest exaggerations that I ended up using in the speech: *senior moments* became *sabbaticals, driving slowly* became *getting passed by the guy mowing the median,* and *the good old days* became the *Spanish American War*.

Self-Directed Humor - This is another easy style of humor to master because no one understands you better than you do. Make a list of the things family and friends tease you about. Write down physical and personality attributes that characterize you. Then use exaggeration, the rule of three, or any of the other humor styles to change your perspective and see the humor in your situation.

For example, let's say you are short and get teased about it often. Make a list of the types of remarks about your height that make you or others laugh out loud, including all of the humorous disadvantages of being short, then rewrite these comments and observations from your perspective so they will get even bigger laughs. As a result, you might come up with, "I can live with being short, but I hate having to wear my younger brother's hand-me-downs!"

Remember, the easiest way to disarm your critics and tormentors is to beat them to the punch. As we have stressed, self-directed humor endears you to others and let's them know that you are self-confident enough to kid yourself.

Combinations - A humorous effect can be achieved by combining two disparate ideas that the audience does not see. I write a speaker-oriented humor column for several publications, and one of my themes was *Country Music Song Titles Inspired by Toastmasters*.

To flesh out this idea, I made two columns: one column contained Toastmasters-related expressions and quirks, and the other column contained popular country and western song titles. I then looked at ways to combine these two themes into one. This led to song titles such as *Achy Breaky Slide Projector*, *By the Time I Get To My Conclusion You'll be Gone*, and *I Never Knew Lonely Until My First Joke Bombed!*

Try this exercise using two different themes. Perhaps you are a blonde and a professional speaker. Write down all the stereotypes of being blonde as well as a speaker, then, using combinations and self-directed humor, you might come up with lines like, "I was half-way through my speech and the audience started booing the previous speaker. Can they do that?" Or, "I got my notes out of order recently and started my speech, *In conclusion...*"

Become a Student

To really study the art of creating original humor, I recommend signing up to receive John Kinde's online *Humor Power* newsletter at *www.humorpower.com*. If you google *Creating Original Humor*, his great article on the subject comes up. Another excellent resource is the book *Comedy Writing Secrets by Melvin Helitzer*. Also, entering contests will expand your sense of humor.

Becoming a student of humor helps you internalize the necessary skills to recognize humorous connections and relationships when they appear. Part of the learning process involves failure...trying to be funny and missing the target. Don't get discouraged, and don't overthink it. The longer you analyze humor, the less funny it may seem.

Stage Time

In Toastmasters, members have the opportunity to use the organization as a laboratory where they can try new humor, make mistakes, and receive constructive feedback. Often, the feedback will include suggestions for funnier lines or better execution of the humor.

Many serious students of communication and humor belong to multiple Toastmasters clubs. I am personally in two clubs, which enables me to give a speech in one club, receive constructive feedback, make improvements, and then give the improved version of the speech to my other club, where I receive more feedback.

The key to getting better is increased stage time. Never pass up an opportunity to give a speech, presentation, or tell a joke when asked. And keep your eyes and ears open - there is humor everywhere!

(13)
Special Occasions

"Good speakers are in great demand. Once you have learned to tell stories well, you will be invited to speak at a wide variety of special occasions."

- Winston K. Pendleton

As you become a more entertaining speaker, your popularity will increase and so will your reputation. Organizers of special events will invite you to serve as the master of ceremonies, keynote speaker, roastmaster or roaster, or in some other capacity for the purpose of adding entertainment to the occasion.

Of course, every opportunity to speak should be considered a special occasion. As a keynote speaker, you should always attempt to add several minutes of humor that harmonizes with the particular group or the purpose of its meeting.

If you have a signature speech that doesn't change much from one venue to another, such as my humorous keynote talk *Laugh at Yourself, Others Are*, you can always warm up your audience and connect with them using *housekeeping humor* as described in Chapter Two.

But what about themed meetings like a celebrity roast, sales awards banquet, retirement ceremony, wedding, high school graduation, etc.? These events may require more than the usual customization of your signature talk, or even a mostly new presentation altogether! And as the master of ceremonies or roastmaster at a special event, you will need to work closely with your event coordinator to develop the script and order of events.

Let's look at a few of the more challenging assignments you may be requested to handle...

Master of Ceremonies

The master of ceremonies at an event is like the ringmaster at the circus. As the MC, your role is not to be the star of the show, but to bring out the stars and help them shine! My wife reminded me of that once as I was preparing to assume my MC duties at an important sales banquet. She leaned over to me and whispered into my ear, "Now don't go up there and try to be witty, charming, or intellectual...just be yourself!"

Actually, you should at least be witty and charming as the master of ceremonies. You are a facilitator that creates through your preparation, enthusiasm, and humor, an atmosphere of interest, expectation, excitement, and entertainment. The most important aspect of an MC's persona is personality and charisma. An MC needs to be able to sway and excite the audience while knowing when to pass the baton on to the next program participant.

The leadership and organizational insights you gain from this experience will carry over into other responsibilities where you must coordinate events, keep things moving, entertain an audience, and build anticipation for the scheduled program participants. And of course, MCs are most effective when they are able to add *observational humor* (Chapter 2), as well as planned humor, to the festivities.

Preparation is Key - The assignment as master of ceremonies requires careful preparation in order to have a smoothly running meeting. Check with each speaker or presenter on the program at least a week in advance to obtain biographical information for their introductions. Now, most novice MCs think that the more famous the speaker...the longer the introduction should be! Ironically, it's just the opposite! For example, our nation's Chief Executive is introduced simply, "Ladies and Gentlemen, the President of the United States!"

I learned this rule of thumb the hard way during the early '80s when I had the responsibility of introducing Art Linkletter to the Orlando Sales and Marketing Executives. I had worked for weeks on my introduction of this famous personality, and finally, the big night arrived. There I was, sitting at the head table, reviewing my big stack of notes, when Mr. Linkletter leaned over to me and said, "Karl, you just tell 'em I'm here, *I'll* give the speech!"

The more experienced speakers will usually have their own prepared introductions that they will provide you, but quite often, these will be too long and read more like resumes. You will need to use your organizational and writing skills to pare these manuscripts down to a less tedious length. An introduction is like a mini-speech, preferably less than a minute in length, which contains all the elements of a full speech.

For example, it has an opening in which you immediately and clearly state the speaker's name and make the audience aware of the importance of the speaker's presence and topic. In the body, your introduction should tell the audience about the expertise of the speaker and give relevant background information, but usually only that which applies to the topic. The conclusion is the climactic build-up to actually presenting the speaker with enthusiasm and leading the applause.

One mistake MCs often make is thinking that saving the speaker's name to the last moment of the introduction builds suspense. The problem is that if the name is mumbled, or a distraction occurs at the wrong time, the audience may miss the name of the speaker. You should clearly say the speaker's name early in the introduction, and again at the end.

In Chapter Nine, *Win Them Over Early,* the idea of adding humor to the prepared introduction was discussed as a way to build even more excitement and good will for the speaker. In that chapter was an example of a succinct yet informative introduction. Rehearse the introductions in advance, making sure you know how the participants' names are pronounced. Coordinate with your event coordinator to confirm and finalize the full agenda.

Introducing the Program Participants - This is your most important responsibility! When it comes time to introduce a program participant, your professionalism and enthusiasm will largely determine the level of applause that is generated. A poorly delivered introduction will dig a hole from which any speaker will have a tough time emerging. Remain at the lectern until the speaker has taken his or her position and recognized you, then be seated. Never leave the lectern unattended while you are the master of ceremonies.

At the end of each presentation, lead the applause and offer a brief word of appreciation. Your role as MC is to bridge the gap between presentations, maintaining the momentum, the excitement, and the attention of the audience.

You may also be asked to recognize and introduce the dignitaries sitting at the head table. This is a frequently botched responsibility in two ways: 1) The MC will often just say the person's name and not mention why they are at the head table. Always indicate their title or role on the program, not just their name. You can't assume everyone in the audience knows these dignitaries. 2) Another blunder is introducing the next person before letting the applause for the previous dignitary die down. When you do this, the applause for the previous celebrity will drown out the name of the next person you are trying to recognize, which is a real disservice to that person. It takes a little discipline to learn not to rush through this responsibility.

Incorporating Humor - The best MCs know how to entertain an audience while keeping the program moving briskly along. A couple of minutes of *housekeeping humor* in the opening is the easiest way to immediately connect with the audience, build expectations, and get your program off to a fast start. *Observational humor* gleaned from preceding events can also be used once you become adept at recognizing the opportunities and smoothly inserting those laughs into your prepared remarks. Here's a warm-up routine I delivered as master of ceremonies at a regional Toastmasters conference banquet in 2001:

> *Ken, thanks for that gracious introduction! Sometimes these introductions don't turn out the way you hope. I spoke recently to a church singles group in downtown Orlando. Since they had no budget for a speaker, I agreed to waive my usual fee.*
>
> *So when the program chairperson introduced me, she said, "Our guest speaker this evening is Karl Righter, an author and professional speaker. Our committee was hesitant to invite someone of Mr. Righter's calibre*

to address our small group. In fact, we tried to find someone less distinguished for this occasion, but we couldn't!"

Well, we do have a distinguished group of dignitaries at this head table. Sitting up here with all these celebrities has been a little overwhelming. I just realized a few minutes ago as I looked around up here that I'm the only one at this head table I've never heard of!

We should definitely thank someone for the fine dinner we had tonight! I certainly enjoyed mine! There was a time, however, when I wouldn't eat before a big speech or assignment such as this. Many years ago in Tampa I was the keynote speaker at a big event. My steak dinner was sitting in front of me getting cold, and the program chairperson leaned over and said, "Karl, aren't you hungry tonight?" I replied, "I am hungry, but I've heard that you shouldn't eat right before you have to do something cerebral because all the oxygen leaves your head to assist with the digestive process, and I need to be mentally sharp tonight!" Later, after I gave my speech and returned to my seat, the program chairperson leaned over again and said, "You could have just as well eaten the steak!"

Well, I ate the steak tonight, and for good reason. Like the food, this entire conference has been a success in every way, and what a wonderful hotel for this event! We certainly didn't have anything this fancy during my year as District Governor! One of my conferences was at a motel in South Florida called the Apollo Inn. This place was so cheezy that the beds weren't even made up on their picture post cards!

At this point, having warmed up the audience with some self-deprecating humor, I began the formal part of the program and introduced the first speaker. Notice the use of *housekeeping humor* to reference my introduction, the food, the head table, and the hotel venue. Also note the segues I used to move smoothly from one laugh to the next. If there is an event theme, such as an awards celebration, retirement ceremony, officer installation, etc., try to interject snappy, related humor throughout the program as a way of keeping the audience entertained and insuring continuity. One funny quip between each part of the program should suffice. You may also use these transitional opportunities to add *observational humor* based on a remark or activity by a previous speaker.

The Celebrity Roast

"The roast is based on the ironic premise that a celebrity can be honored through the recognition, exaggeration, and public announcement of all his faults, real or imagined," wrote Ed McManus, co-author with Bill Nicholas of *We're Roasting Harry Tuesday Night*. He continues, "The roast assumes that the guest of honor would rather be recognized through this controlled hostility than not be recognized at all."

Audiences certainly love roasts. As comic Joey Adams once put it, "If you can't say anything nice...let's hear it!" The celebrity roast is considered to be a positive way to pay tribute to the guest of honor, targeting for comic effect through jokes and stories his or her accomplishments, gaffes, and eccentricities. Ideally, these anecdotes are neither harmful, nor necessarily true, but are hopefully entertaining and not humiliating.

Any of the 25 types of humor discussed in Chapter Two can be used in a celebrity roast. Of particular effectiveness are *one-liners, exaggeration and understatement, satire, parody*, and *observational humor*. As always, off-color or blue material is never appropriate at any type of meeting or event.

Sample Roast - Here is an example of my roast of the Orange County Tax Collector, Earl K. Wood, on the occasion in 2006 of his 50th anniversary as a member of the Orlando Toastmasters Club:

We're here this evening to pay tribute to a legendary Toastmaster, exemplary family man, and inspirational leader. Unfortunately, Past International Director Paul Meunier could not attend this evening, so we're roasting Earl K. Wood instead.

I'm honored to pay my respects to Earl this evening, because I've been around some great Toastmasters over the years, and so has Earl.

Earl and I go back a long way, although Earl goes back a lot further. He remembers, for example, when the Dead Sea was only ill, and Florida was still owned by Spain.

Earl Wood was actually born in 1916 and recently celebrated his 90th birthday. This guy is older than dirt! He has soup stains on his tie older than me!

When Earl was a teenager, he had a lot of charisma. Then he discovered girls. His charisma cleared up, but his face didn't.

Earl says there are a lot of advantages of being old. No peer pressure, cougars don't pester him any more, and he can hide his own Easter eggs.

Just keep an eye on your drink when he's nearby. I set my glass of water down a few minutes ago and he dropped his teeth in it.

Note that all of the previous quips are good-natured fun, not brutal or humiliating. There is a fine line between the two, and when you are a roaster for the first time, you should review your proposed material with a veteran of several roasts to insure it is in good taste. In the example above, I knew that jokes about Earl's age were appropriate since he kids himself about his age.

As the roastmaster, a lot of the same guidelines for a master of ceremonies described previously apply to this responsibility. One thing that is crucial to the success of a roast is selecting funny speakers. Over the years, I have seen boring speakers picked to be on the program because they are close friends of the honoree or they want a payback for some reason. This is no time for favors... you want the best roasters available. Rehearsal is also critical to get the timing right, eliminate duplicate gags, and weed out weak or offensive material. Keep in mind that the roastee has the last word, a chance for rebuttal, so you need to let him or her know who the roasters are so a measured response can be planned ahead of time.

The Rebuttal - When you are the roastee, you have the advantage of having the last word, and if you are already a gifted humorist, or at least a student of the game and do your homework, your response could end up being the highlite of the event. A couple of jabs at each of your tormentors, followed by your heartfelt thanks for the honor of the tribute, can tie the perfect bow around an entertaining event. Be gracious, and be appreciative. Remember, they don't have celebrity roasts for people who are irrelevant, so consider it one of the highest honors you can receive from your peers.

Here is part of my rebuttal from a recent celebrity roast honoring my 31 years as a roaster or roastmaster at district Toastmasters conferences:

> Wow! I believe this qualifies as elder abuse. And to think I could have had a root canal today instead of coming here and enduring roastmaster Bill and the seven dwarfs!

> Normally these roasts are fun, but today, it seemed like some practical joker got ahold of your scripts and whited out all the punch lines!

> Jordan, you tore a page right out of Roy's joke book today, which left him with nothing, and it didn't help you either!

> Margaret, you've never been funnier than you were today, which is a shame.

> Greg (bald as a gourd), what an honor to be roasted by the Tidy Bowl Man! (this was a line from my club's roast)

> Sandy, I love your hair...don't ever fix it! She's no dumb blonde, folks, I've seen her roots! (Dean Martin's classic line)

> Ron, you missed at least three good opportunities to sit down today. This is no surprise. Ron doesn't smoke or drink, and there's no evidence that he's ever used performance enhancing drugs either!

> Thanks, Linda, for your kind remarks. Linda sure knows the secret of making people laugh! And Linda, your secret is still safe!

Note the short, snappy one-liners, all prepared in advance. By the time you get up for your rebuttal, it has probably been a long, possibly tedious event, depending upon the calibre and long-windedness of the roasters, so you need to keep your response short and entertaining.

The Contest Speech

Toastmasters International has two significant speech contests each year...the World Championship of Public Speaking (also called the International Speech Contest), and the Humorous Speech Contest. In the early years of the World Championship, the speeches were predominantly motivational or inspirational with minimal humor, whereas the Humorous Speech Contest was just that, a competition featuring very funny talks.

Since then, the line between these two contests has become blurred. Recent winners of the World Championship have given very entertaining speeches that could just as easily have won the Humorous Speech Contest. As is the case in the arena of professional speaking, humor is thus becoming an absolute requirement for the speech contestant. Accordingly, if you are serious about becoming a more entertaining speaker, you should absolutely enter every speech contest to hone your skills and develop your funny bone! Stage time, stage time, stage time!

Once you make the decision to compete, your next challenge is deciding on a topic. William H. Stevenson, III, a freelance writer and Toastmaster, says, "Comedians have always known that if you poke fun at yourself, people will laugh. Often all you need to do is exaggerate actual events a little, and sometimes the simplest ideas are the funniest." In other words, if you don't know where to look for material, look in the mirror!

John Zimmer, an attorney in Geneva, Switzerland, drew on marital interaction for his theme in the Annual Toastmasters Humorous Speech Contest and won the District 59 competition. Zimmer recommends choosing topics that audiences can identify with, such as relationships, raising children, financial issues, moving to another home, awkward travel experiences, etc. But be aware that these topics are common. "The challenge is to come up with a unique angle," Zimmer says.

Once you have a workable theme, use as many of the 25 types of humor styles (Chapter Two) as possible to approach the topic from a variety of different perspectives. A proven technique, combining two illogical premises (such as comparing marriage to the Olympics), can be a very funny approach.

As an example, following is the script for a speech I used to win the Division Humorous Speech Contest for Toastmasters International in 1996. It combines one plausible theme, a joint business venture with my brother, with a parody on an imaginary government subsidy program. The idea resonated with many in the audience who have known friends or family members that botched a business opportunity:

A Pig in a Poke

I never really wanted to be a hog farmer! I was trained in the computer business! But one day, back in the fall of '83, my brother called me on the phone, all excited, and said, "I found it!" I said, "Found what?" "The perfect business...one that pays us for doing nothing!" I said, "I'm already doing nothing for my present employer!" He said, "Yea, and you're being paid accordingly! Why not join the proud work force of 20 million Americans who do nothing for the government! After all, the government's doing nothing for us!" He added, "All we need is one hog and a small piece of land to qualify for the new Government Hog Subsidy Program!"

"The what?" "The GHSP! The government will pay us for not raising hogs! And the more we don't raise, the bigger the subsidy!" I said, "We can do that!"

So my brother and I pooled our life savings, not to mention our total lack of business acumen, and bought the farm...literally...a small, one-hog farm in Bithlo, Florida! Bithlo was not the end of the world, but you could see it from there!

Now, you'd think that getting paid to do nothing would be a piece of cake, but we had all kinds of problems! Our hog business turned out to be a "pig in a poke!"

Now, for you city slickers, a 'pig in a poke' is a pig dressed up in a bonnet...in other words, an opportunity that looks better than it really is! And this hog subsidy business was a classic example!

1) The first problem...we couldn't decide on a name for our hog farm. We considered..."Southpork." Then we tried "Hog Heaven." Finally we decided on the glaringly obvious choice, "Hogs Aren't Us!"

2) The next challenge was trying to set business objectives! My brother said, "Karl, how many hogs do you reckon we ought not to raise this year?" "Well, we need to start out slow," I replied. "Maybe we ought not raise 100 the first year!"

3) So we had a goal, but then we had another problem...staying motivated! How do you get pumped up to do nothing? We tried watching C-Span to see how the bureaucrats did it, but that didn't help much!

I remember one afternoon asking my brother, who was our VP of sales, "How's your week going?" He said, "Well, Monday, I didn't sell two hogs because, obviously, we don't have two hogs! Tuesday, nothing happened. And today, my deal from Monday fell through! I guess you'd have to say Tuesday was my best day so far this week!"

Another problem: the one hog we did have, Portabella, was eating us out of house and farm...a real pig! We really needed that first subsidy check!

But fortunately, our goal of not raising 100 hogs the first year was realistic, and we achieved it! Sure enough, a government agent came out to our little hog farm and gave us our first subsidy check! We were so excited! Now we could really start living high on the hog, so to speak!

So I said to my brother, "Well, how many hogs do you reckon we ought not to raise next year?" He said, "We should be able to not raise 200 hogs as easily as we didn't raise 100. Let's go for 200!" So we doubled our quota, and once again, we kicked hog butt! And just as before, a *government agent came out to our little hog farm and gave us another check! We had indeed found the perfect business!*

So I said, "Pete, how many hogs do you reckon we ought not to raise next year?" "I think we should expand," he replied. "We should be able to not raise a thousand hogs as easily as we didn't raised two hundred!" I said, "You're right! Let's go for it!"

Well, this tale has a sad ending. We tried to expand too fast and lost our shirts! How depressing that was! It's pretty humiliating to be getting paid to do nothing and screw that up!

What was even worse, Portabella was getting larger, and larger, and eating more, and more! One day, I was out walking around our farm and I saw my brother hoisting Portabella up in the air so she could eat apples off one of the apple trees! I said, "What in the heck are you doing?"

He said, "We're out of money! We're out of hog feed! These apples are all we have left to feed her!" I said, "Yea, but isn't that terribly time-consuming?" "Sure," he replied, "but what's time to a dumb hog?"

I thought a lot about his reply that day... "What's time to a dumb hog? Or, for that matter, to a couple of guys trying to get something for nothing!"

Not long after that, the government ended the Hog Subsidy Program, and since it no longer made sense for us to not raise hogs, we sold the farm! And from that day on, my brother and I have been very wary of any deals that sound too good to be true! Because you never know when it might be a "pig in a poke!"

Note that this speech contained a lot of dialogue between my brother and me. Dialogue allows for emotions to surface much more easily than in a monologue, and humor unfolds as the emotions of the characters change and evolve. In the speech, I also used exaggerated voice inflection, facial expressions, and gestures to act out each scene and convey the irony of trying to get something for nothing.

The outline above is a good template for a contest speech. Try your hand at developing a humorous speech. Obviously, this type of presentation is not bombproof because the audience knows what the intent of the contest is, but by continuing to work at humor and entering these contests, you will become a funnier speaker!

Giving a Toast

Many of life's special occasions call for a toast. If you are selected to give one, the challenge of doing so with style, sincerity, eloquence, and humor can be challenging.

Maybe you've been asked to raise a glass of champagne and deliver a tribute at your best friend's wedding. Or perhaps your company's CEO is retiring and you have been asked to say a few words. You will usually be given advanced notice that you will be called upon for a tribute, but on many other occasions, you will need to anticipate situations in which you are an obvious choice to give a toast, such as when you are a very close friend or relative of the person being honored, or are a well-known celebrity. Whatever the occasion, you need to be prepared in the event your name is called. This means research, preparation, and practice.

Just as you are not the star when serving as the master of ceremonies, your toast should be about the person you are honoring and not about how clever or funny you are. Your toast needs to be succinct, sincere, and upbeat.

A toast is like a mini-speech that is hopefully both complimentary and entertaining. You will want to begin by addressing the honoree by name, mention your connection to them for the benefit of those at the event who don't know you, note a few relevant accomplishments or qualities, possibly share a humorous personal story, and conclude by leading the toast.

As with the celebrity roast, there is a fine line between a tribute and public humiliation. This comes into particular play at a wedding when you are asked to give a toast to the bride, groom, best man, or maid or matron of honor. If there is any doubt about how a planned remark may be received by the honoree, leave it out.

Here is a toast I gave to the best man at my brother's wedding rehearsal:

I offer a toast to Greg, my brother's best man, who has been Pete's closest friend since they were in college. Over the years, Greg has always been there for my brother, but on this wonderful occasion, he is confused about his designation as the best man. He said to me, "If I'm the best man, why is she marrying him?" So, here's to Greg, who tomorrow will be dressed in the same style tuxedo as the groom, ready to be a true friend and take one step right if called upon. Here, here!

Note that this toast meets all of the criteria for a good tribute as outlined above...it begins by addressing the best man by name, reveals my connection to the proceedings as Pete's brother, notes an admirable quality of Greg's, includes a humorous observation, and concludes by leading the tribute.

Once again, the Internet is your friend. For example, if you google *Wedding Toasts,* you will pull up over 350,000 sources! You can also find resources on-line for when you have to give the very important *Father of the Bride* speech or other requested tribute.

Remember, your toast should leave the honoree, and everyone else, feeling better for your efforts.

Giving a Eulogy

It's no easy task summing up someone's life in just a few words, especially if you are extremely close to the deceased and emotionally impacted by the loss of this cherished soul. To make this responsibility easier for you as well as the bereaved, try to make this an upbeat celebration of the person's life rather than focusing on the tragedy of the loss.

There is an incorrect perception that humor is not appropriate in a eulogy. However, remember that we have discussed how humor can break the tension in a speech and lift the audience back up again. Nowhere is this more important than in a eulogy, which is prone to heavy sentiment and anguish. Mixing positive stories about the person's life with humorous remembrances makes for an uplifting tribute to the deceased.

According to author Tom Chiarella, Visiting Professor of Creative Writing at DePauw University, "Laughs are a pivot point in a funeral. They are your responsibility. The best laughs come by not forcing people to idealize the dead. In order to do this, you have to be willing to tell a story, at the closing of which you draw conclusions that no one expects."

Here is an excerpt from a tribute I paid to a beloved member of our Toastmasters club, Cameron Lusk, after his tragic death at a young age:

Cameron Lusk was one of the most enthusiastic Toastmasters I ever knew. He was called "Mr. Enthusiasm," and he made Zig Ziglar seem like a sedated Ed Sullivan.

Cam served as president in 1988, leading us to Distinguished Club status, but rather than fade away as many past presidents have done, he continued to give everything he had to our club for three more years until his untimely death.

Vince Lombardi demanded 110% from his players...Cam gave it without being asked. His energy was contagious and always over-the-top. If you needed a Toastmaster of the evening, he gave you an entertaining game show host. If you needed violins, you got a marching band. If you needed an invocation, you got Billy Graham channeling General Patton. Most of all, if you needed a friend you could depend on, he gave you himself.

Note that these remarks attempt to balance Cameron's endearing qualities with a mild sense of exaggeration for humorous effect to keep the proceedings light and alleviate the tension and sense of loss.

Read Tom Chiarella's on-line article, *How to Give a Eulogy* (2006), for some remarkable insights into this ultimate speaking challenge and responsibility.

Speaking to Young Audiences

It is a challenge to connect with a young audience today. In this age of Twitter and text messaging, young adults have short attention spans and need short, snappy ideas and humor to hold their attention.

As Win Pendleton once wrote, "Remember that youngsters today don't usually laugh at the same stories you enjoyed when you were a kid. Changes in vocabulary and differences in style of living account for this. Use a few of their latest pet words and phrases and you will build a quick and solid rapport with your audience. Make sure, though, that you keep abreast of the current slang expressions. You can improve your chances of success if you listen to the local radio disc jockey or watch one of the weekly television teen shows." Good advice in Win's day...still good advice.

Here are some examples of the type of short quips that may work with young adults:

My daughter came home from school today and said the teacher handed out mystery books to the class. I asked her what was the title of the book? She said, 'Second-Year Algebra.'

When my daughter's cat died recently, I had a hard time comforting her. After many attempts to get her to stop crying, I finally said, "Jessie's in a better place. She's gone to be with God." To which my daughter replied, "What does God want with a dead cat?"

I recently asked my Sunday School class, "How many of you kids want to go to heaven?" All of them raised their hands except little Jimmy. "What about you, Jimmy? Don't you want to go to heaven when you die?" "Yea, when I die," he replied. "I thought you were trying to get up a group to go right now!"

When a family moved into their new house, a visiting relative asked the little five-year-old how he liked the new place. "It's terrific," he said. "I have my own room, my brother has his own room, and my sister has her own room. But poor mom is still sleeping with dad."

Religious Groups

Using humor when speaking to a religious affiliation is a little tricky. The humor certainly can't put down the religion, and its members have probably already heard most of the generic jokes. You may want to review your planned humor with the program chairperson who invited you to speak.

A good idea is to research comedians who appeal to the followers of that religion, and try to pick up ideas, themes, and techniques that seem to work well. Following is a warm-up routine I used at a Jewish social club meeting to which I was invited to give my humorous keynote talk *Laugh at Yourself, Others Are*. I got the idea for my first story from a routine used by Rabbi Bob Alper, a Jewish stand-up comedian. As I teach in Chapter 7, *Make it Believable*, I rewrote and personalized Alper's idea for my first laugh. For the follow-up, I shared one of Alper's funniest stories. Here is how I opened my talk:

Thank you for that kind introduction, and for the invitation to visit with you this afternoon. This isn't my first exposure to your religion. A Jewish member of my Toastmasters club recently invited me to attend a Friday evening Shabbat service at Congregation Ohev Shalom. This particular service happened to be mostly in Yiddish, so I wasn't sure what was going on. I decided to do whatever the gentleman seated next to me did. When he would stand, I would stand. When he would sit, I would sit.

Toward the end of the service, the Rabbi said something in Yiddish, the gentleman seated next to me stood up, I stood up, and everybody started laughing, pointing, and giggling. I looked around and noticed that no one else was standing. Later I found out that the embarrassing incident happened during a baby-naming ceremony, and the Rabbi had asked, "Will the father of the baby please stand."

As a humorist, I enjoy listening to stand-up comedians. One of my favorites is Rabbi Bob Alper (that's right, he's a Rabbi!). I notice quite a few of you have heard of him. He likes to tell the story of a Jewish gentleman whose daughter was the apple of his eye. When it came time for her to go away to college, she announced that she was going to attend the University of Colorado to study Indian lore. Needless to say, about this idea, her father had "reservations!" Sure enough, six months later, he received a letter from his daughter advising him that she had met a wonderful Native American man and they were to be married. The father was devastated. He no longer had a daughter and cut off all contact.

Four years later, he received another letter from his daughter. She said she and her husband were very happily married and had just welcomed a new son into their life. She said they had given the baby a Jewish name. Well, the father's heart melted. He got on the first plane and flew to Colorado. When he got off the plane, he and his daughter hugged, they embraced, they wept, and tears of joy streamed down their faces. Then the daughter picked up their new baby and said, "Father, this is your new grandson...Whitefish."

Note that the first rewritten humorous story employed bombproof self-deprecating humor, and the second story was credited to a Jewish Rabbi, thus insuring that both stories would be well received, which they were. As you become more adept at using humor, you will see such opportunities for laughs in so many different situations.

Other Special Events

Just about any special event requires the same strategies...preparation, good speakers, targeted messages and humor, brisk pacing, self-deprecating laughs, and theme continuity throughout the program. As previously mentioned, it's not hard to find topical humor on the Internet for such occasions. For example, if you are asked to serve as the keynote speaker at a sales awards banquet, humor about the profession of selling is a must. Google *sales profession jokes* and you will have over 3.5 million sources to choose from. Are you scheduled to serve as the master of ceremonies at a retirement dinner for a corporate legend? Google *retirement jokes* and you will have over half-a-million sources to choose from.

Yes, every opportunity to speak, give a toast or eulogy, or serve as a master of ceremonies should be treated as a special occasion. And stage time is the only way you will get better, funnier, and more professional. Learn to master *bombproof humor,* and as you improve, you will find yourself more and more in demand. That will be pretty special as well!

About the Author

In 1980, Karl Righter of Orlando won Toastmasters International's Humorous Speech Contest at the highest level with a hilarious talk entitled *Laugh at Yourself, Others Are*. His message was simple - that the ability to laugh at ourselves is crucial to our sanity during life's inevitable tough times. This achievement launched his professional speaking career.

Since then, Karl Righter has been entertaining and inspiring audiences as a keynote speaker, corporate trainer, master of ceremonies, roastmaster, humorist, musician, and published author.

For over 25 years, he has presented his humor workshop, *How To Win Your Audience With Bombproof Humor*, to thousands of attendees at district, regional, and international Toastmasters conventions as well as at public workshops and seminars.

In 2001, Karl Righter was presented with a Presidential Citation for Lifetime Achievement at the Toastmasters International Convention in Anaheim, California. His humor columns have appeared in a variety of publications for over 20 years, including *Toastmaster Magazine*.

For information regarding bookings for keynote speeches, workshops, coaching, speech writing, or other special events, e-mail Karl Righter at karl@righter.com.

Righter Entertainment
www.RighterEntertainment.com
Contact: karl@righter.com
321-356-4129
copyright 2010

Made in the USA
Charleston, SC
21 August 2012